THE POWER OF
PERSUASION

THE POWER OF PERSUASION

Techniques to **INFLUENCE** Anyone and Everyone

Rudy Nash

Published by
Rupa Publications India Pvt. Ltd 2022
7/16, Ansari Road, Daryaganj
New Delhi 110002

Sales centres:
Allahabad Bengaluru Chennai
Hyderabad Jaipur Kathmandu
Kolkata Mumbai

Copyright © Rudy Nash 2022

The views and opinions expressed in this book are the
author's own and the facts are as reported by him which
have been verified to the extent possible, and the publishers
are not in any way liable for the same.

All rights reserved.
No part of this publication may be reproduced, transmitted,
or stored in a retrieval system, in any form or by any means,
electronic, mechanical, photocopying, recording or otherwise,
without the prior permission of the publisher.

ISBN: 9978-81-291-4192-7

First impression 2022

10 9 8 7 6 5 4 3 2 1

The moral right of the author has been asserted.

Printed in India

This book is sold subject to the condition that it shall not,
by way of trade or otherwise, be lent, resold, hired out, or otherwise
circulated, without the publisher's prior consent, in any form of
binding or cover other than that in which it is published.

CONTENTS

1. Understand the System — 1
2. Grasp the Language — 11
3. Speak the Style — 26
4. Target the Attitude — 46
5. Meet the Desires — 64
6. Don't Question; Find Out — 82
7. Emotion Is the Key — 99
8. Expectation and Experience — 112
9. Add Style and Art — 120
10. The Personal Touch — 132

Conclusion — 139

I

UNDERSTAND THE SYSTEM

Noted actor and filmmaker Laurence Olivier had an insightful comment on the power of persuasion. He said, 'The actor persuades himself first, and through himself, the audience.' Olivier was very right. If an actor does not believe in the character he is portraying, he will fail to credibly project it; and the audience will, in turn, not be convinced by the act.

This is true of any profession or behavioural conduct. You seek to persuade your boss in the office that you are both overworked and underpaid; you want to persuade your spouse that you are not neglecting the family in pursuit of your career; you may wish to persuade your child not to binge on chocolates; or you want to persuade your friend that he or she has got you all wrong.

Global leaders meet at conferences or one-on-one and are eager to persuade the other to see their point of reasoning. Persuasion to apply or not to apply sanctions, to extend monetary credit on easy terms or even to avoid conflicts and bloodshed.

It is often believed that the power to persuade is inbuilt in some people. Nothing could be more wrong. Persuasion is both an art and a science and has to be understood to be applied effectively. Not everybody is a persuader—which is why persuasion fails so often. Most people can be good persuaders if they follow some simple rules. This book is about those secrets that make for potent persuasive powers.

We have to acknowledge that many decisions that we make are grounded in spontaneous thought processes and less rooted in scientific material at hand. Consciousness does not occupy a central place in our thinking—at least most of the times—which is why, most of the times, we make wrong decisions that we have instances to reflect with regret at our leisure. Human resource managers across the world spend hours analysing successes and failures of employees. They dwell on a person's work hours, ability to grasp issues, compatibility with co-workers and their willingness to accept orders and implement them. Rarely does the HR manager strive to understand the inner functioning of the mind. That is, thankfully, changing—though slowly. HR evaluation is getting focused on ways the mind works, and through that understanding, the evaluator is able to not just understand but also make course-corrections.

Through progress in science, we are now better placed to have insights on the mind and to apply them to the art of persuasion. No longer is persuasion a hit-or-miss exercise; if approached with precision, it cannot fail. We have a number of expert studies to assist us in the matter. For instance, Daniel Kahneman, the Israeli psychologist and economist known for his deep study of decision-making and for which received the Nobel Prize in 2002, teamed up with fellow Israeli and cognitive and mathematical psychologist Amos Tversky to publish a series of articles on judgement and decision-making.

The techniques they laid down are not merely theoretical; they help us understand decision-making processes in human beings and their cognitive skills—including persuasive powers.

The insights can help the salesman who is striving to convince a reluctant customer to opt for a MacBook instead of a less expensive rival brand or a businessman who is hoping to persuade the bank manager to part with a hefty loan for his new enterprise.

Ways We Think

There are two broad ways in which we think. The reflective and the automatic. The first derives from an analysis of the pros and cons and goes beyond what is apparent or seems obvious. The automatic way, on the other hand, is what the non-conscious mind decides. We talk, walk and do our daily chores like an automaton, without consciously evaluating the acts. Often, in a similar manner, we evolve our likes and dislikes and general reflexes. We don't have to think that it will hurt us to touch a thorn; we know it automatically. There is no conscious deliberation involved.

In his book, *Strangers to Ourselves,* author Timothy Wilson writes, 'We do not realize how much the non-conscious mind impacts our behaviour and personality. In many cases, the non-conscious mind influences our behaviour more than our conscious thoughts do and the two minds will often conflict with one another, which can make it difficult to keep our desires and our actions in alignment. The first step to bringing our non-conscious inclinations into alignment with our conscious desires is to act more like the person we want to be.'[1]

Following the automatic route results in a partial understanding of issues at hand, and the persuasion that rests on that little understanding is more likely to fail. If the reader

---

[1] Timothy D Wilson, *Strangers to Ourselves*, Harvard University Press, 2004.

thinks that this is all leading to the dumping of emotional responses and the predominance of the rational, the impression needs a correction. On the contrary, a better understanding of the mind's operation will help in leveraging emotional responses to one's benefit. Why must I buy a particular brand of low-cholesterol cooking oil over another rival brand? Scientific jargon alone will not work; in any case, both brands would flout it. Emotional stirrings, like those of health and wellbeing of loved ones, will work.

There are many things that we don't indulge in normally, because they are part of our non-conscious process. For instance, we don't usually sit back and evaluate the various religions and choose the best suited for us. We do not study a bunch of associates to determine who would make a good friend. Religion is what we inherit from our parents, and friends are made intuitively. The choices were made without any of us understanding what led to those choices.

Most experts working in the field of psychology, cognitive behaviour and decision-making processes agree that the consciousness is not central to most of our thought processes. By extension, the process of persuasion too falls prey to the non-conscious. Austrian neurologist and founder of psychoanalysis (a clinical method to understand the behaviour of humans,) Sigmund Freud was the first to focus attention on the subject. While some of his theories and findings have since been disproved by later studies, his contribution to understanding the non-conscious and the conscious continue to be relevant to date. He had remarked, 'Unexpressed emotions will never die. They are buried alive and will come forth later in uglier ways.' The persuasive mind will find ways to get those hidden emotions out and channel them in positive ways.

The reflective and the automatic systems exist side by side, and there is no clear demarcation when they are put in motion. However, the automatic system is predominant is most spheres of our functioning, and it literally keeps us alive—our biological functions such as the way we breathe, the way the heart pumps blood, the way our digestive system takes care of our health, etc. We need to find that right balance between the reflective and the automatic, but to do that, we have to understand how the automatic system works. This will also assist us thereafter in the craft of persuasion.

What, then, are the major distinguishing elements in the two ways of our thinking? The reflective or conscious system is deliberate and takes its own time, involves effort, takes a long-term perspective and has the flexibility to adapt to new evidences and learn new tasks to meet those evidences. On the other hand, the automatic or the non-conscious system works at breakneck speed, proceeds without any apparent effort, reacts on a here-and-now basis, is unintentional, and can make us perform tasks that we are used to and become sort of experts at.

Our automatic system is the one that determines our initial impressions about people. Let's say that we meet a person for the first time. That person's face immediately reveals his pleasure or the lack of it meeting us. That happens in a fleeting moment. Then, that expression is replaced by a more stable, polite one. Our automatic system catches the first impression instantly, but because the second reaction is different, we are left with an ambiguous sense of the person's attitude. Speed, which comes with the automatic system, is necessary to grasp a person's first impression about you.

We can take a real-life example to illustrate this point. You walk into a car showroom with an intention to buy a high-end model. The salesman sees you and walks towards you with a bored expression, which he quickly replaces with a plastered smile. But that quickness is not good enough, because your automatic system has already caught the salesman's disinterest. The car is good and you want to purchase it, but you are put off by the salesman. After a while, you walk out without making the purchase and choose another dealer. Had the salesman been equipped with the techniques of persuasion, he would have behaved differently.

It's not just the expressions on someone's face that catches a person's attention. Sound, smell, taste or other stimuli—and also the language—play a role in determination, in forming judgements and eventually, in matters of persuasion. Scientists today have made enormous progress in understanding these factors, and they have estimated that our reflective system processes as many as 40 different pieces of information per second. Impressive as it sounds, the automatic system does far more—though with less accuracy. Here too, scientists have managed to get an insight through counting the number of nerve connections that send signals to the brain and the signals every nerve sends per second. According to research, all our sense put together transmits more than a million pieces of information every second. It is obvious that the capacity of the automatic system is far larger—by some accounts, more than 20,000 times—than the reflective system. This would have led to chaos but for the fact that our non-conscious system is required to process this large flow of information in such a short time span. The trick it uses is to help us decide on the advantages (or disadvantages) even before those advantages or disadvantages are known to us through a reflective process. Either way, the mind decides advantageously before the advantages are evident.

The other method it uses is to simply leave a good deal of the information unabsorbed. Thus, such materials do not even enter into our consciousness.

Imagine a game of cards in progress. A player had to choose from decks of cards. He flips a card from one deck and loses. He then tries another card from the same deck, and the result is the same. Soon, he begins to avoid that deck because he believes it has risks, though he has no way of knowing that gains could be had from that deck too—if only he continued to play from it. He goes on to another deck, though he does not know that it could be as risky as the other one or less risky for that matter. The automatic system has told him that one is risky and the other, possibly less so.

Conscious thinking, or reflective thinking, needs effort. For example, if one has to multiply 458 with 2397, that calls for some effort and concentration and going through a mathematical process. But one does not need to put in a similar effort to talk in a language one understands. Conversation becomes effortless—in a non-conscious way. The automatic system cannot be switched off; it's always on and comes into the act without any prompting. It's a great mental feat actually. Think of the difficulty you face while trying to converse in a language that you are not adept at and have to form words and sentences in your mind reflectively before speaking. We say 'hello' without having to deliberate on how to say it, but we cannot do calculations without deliberation.

Now imagine that we become an expert, over a period of time and with training, in mathematical calculations. What happens then? We begin to make calculations without much effort or deliberation. In other words, the mind has transferred the task from the reflective to the automatic. This is also true of other cases that become easy for us through practice and become part of the non-conscious process: driving a car, eating with chopsticks, playing the guitar and even writing books.

We often encounter the term 'instant gratification' in our lives. It refers to immediate gains. It is what our automatic mind understands. It does not see the future, only what is here and now. The reflective mind thinks long-term. The automatic system sees the food on the plate, the reflective system visualizes the process of cultivation and harvesting. It is the latter method that gives rise to technological innovations in agriculture.

However critical the reflective system is in the long term, it is the non-conscious that plays the dominant role in crafting our attempts at persuasion. It is for that reason that this book lays extra emphasis on the automatic system.

What Is Persuasion?

Persuasion is an exercise we conduct in order to convince someone to do or say something one may not want to. Conversely, it is to make someone not say or not do something one might want to. Your friend's office is barely a mile away from his home, but he uses a car to commute. He is so used to the car that he cannot think of travelling otherwise. You may wish to make him use a bicycle. A man is determined to call in the police, because he has had a verbal spat with his neighbour. You may want to convince him against the move, because it would further escalate matters. In both cases, the craft of persuasion will be needed.

These may seem like simple enough endeavours, but they are not. You are dealing with people who are determined to stick to their positions. It could be their way of demonstrating their ego or not wanting outside intervention. How do you persuade them?

Often, the presentation of an alternative that does not seek a compromise or the elaboration of the pros and cons can work wonders. The car-driving gentleman can be told of the advantages of using the cycle for short trips—health, savings on fuel, the avoidance of traffic hassles. The man who is ready to involve the police in a small scuffle can be told of the problems that it could lead to in the coming days and weeks, since the establishment of normal relations with his neighbour will become difficult and remain a constant source of tension in his life.

In both the above cases, we are faced with the automatic system at work. Neither the car-using man nor the quarrelling neighbour has thought through their actions, and both are driven by instant impulses. These automatic systems need to be interrupted by the reflective system. I may encounter a person who speaks some nonsense to me. If I can rein in my impulse to ask him to 'get lost', I will have turned my automatic response to a reflective one.

In recent months, some truly creative advertisement campaigns were unleashed in Ireland urging people to wear face masks in the wake of the Covid-19 pandemic. It was a fine example of effective persuasion. In one ad, a young woman was seen wearing a mask, and the text said: 'I'd rather look stupid than be selfish.' Another featured a masked man, with the comment: 'A pain in the face for you. A lifeline for me.' Both the advertisements played on the arguments that people could have for not wearing a mask and sought to persuade them in gentle ways.

The automatic system kicks in spontaneously, but it can take a backseat or retune itself when faced with facts. A man with a cancer condition is told by the doctor that he could take medicine. He would readily agree. If he were to be told that the drugs could possibly not work effectively for long and a better solution would be surgery, he might still waver. But when confronted with statistics that show a higher recovery rate in patients with surgery than with medicines, he could change his mind. If the doctor were to merely talk of risks, with both options having their share of it, the patient would more likely go for medication or radiation. However, when the doctor talks of survival chances, the voice changes dramatically. The craft of persuasion lies, therefore, in how a situation is presented.

Successful persuasion needs dealing with the automatic system. How does one attempt that?

1. Understand the language and tone of the automatic system. It will help in communicating better with a person.
2. Concentrate on emotions. Facts don't change feelings.
3. Don't try to change attitudes but the actual act. Attitude takes a lifelong to change.
4. Don't be interrogative. People do not like being questioned only to be exposed. Talk to them and make them say what you want them to.
5. Offer an alternative experience. That way, people will be able to visualize better and be more amenable to persuasion.
6. Never try to replace desires of people with that of your own in a bid to convince them. Tell them how their desires can be fulfilled in a different way.

2

GRASP THE LANGUAGE

Nelson Mandela had famously said: 'If you talk to a man in a language he understands, that goes to his head. If you talk to him in his language, that goes to his heart.' Language exists not just in the alphabets and sentences. Music has a language too. So does our automatic, non-conscious mental system. And because it is in the spur of the moment, it comes from the heart and not from the head. If you want to persuade a person over a certain type of action, you have to understand the language of his heart—you need to hear it and speak it.

Neurological and psychological research over the last few decades has shown that the language of the automatic system has two key elements: mental readiness and association of ideas. That's the grammar. But language is not just about grammar. There is style too. In our conversations and in writing, different people adopt different styles of expression. They are reflected through action and emotions and demonstrate our likes and dislikes. The success of persuasion depends on how well we understand the language of the automatic system and respond.

Mental Readiness

Mental readiness refers to what springs most easily to the mind. Once that happens, we non-consciously make use of it to evaluate people, ideas and situations. Our automatic system tells us that what we readily assume is true or approximate to the truth. Alain Samson, founder of BehavioralEconomics.com, gives the example of purchasing behaviours of consumers to illustrate the point:

'Think about the last time you purchased a customizable product. Perhaps it was a laptop computer. You may have decided to simplify your decision making by opting for a popular brand or the one you already owned in the past. You may then have visited the manufacturer's website to place your order. But the decision-making process did not stop there, as you now had to customize your model by choosing from different product attributes (processing speed, hard drive capacity, screen size, etc.) and you were still uncertain which features you really needed. At this stage, most technology manufacturers will show a base model with options that can be changed according to the buyer's preferences. The way in which these product choices are presented to buyers will influence the final purchases made and illustrates a number of concepts from behavioural economic (BE) theories.'[2]

He further says that the more uncertain customers are about their decision, the more likely it is that they will choose the default choice—which is the base model of the laptop. Once they are given the full range of choices, the persuasive powers

---

[2] Alain Samson, 'An Introduction to Behavioral Economics', BehavioralEconomics.com, https://www.behavioraleconomics.com/resources/introduction-behavioral-economics/, Accessed on 30 March 2022.

kick in. Issues such as upgradation, price, compatibility, etc. come into play. At the same time, the success of persuasion will depend on making optimum use of the customer's mental readiness.

Ideally, the choice should be influenced not by attractions of price and default models but by a careful evaluation of cost and benefit. But that is not the language—the language of the rational—that the automatic system understands.

In his book, *The Economic Approach to Human Behavior*, the economist Gary S. Becker outlined a number of ideas that are considered the pillars of the rational choice theory. This theory works on the assumption that human beings have stable preferences. Becker applied the rational choice theory to areas ranging from crime to marriage and concluded that academic disciplines such as sociology could learn from the 'rational man' assumption advocated by neoclassical economists since the late nineteenth century.[3]

Mental availability has also to do with the ease of recall. When a person walks into a television showroom, he sees a particular brand and seems to have a memory of it—even if he has not seen that particular brand functional. The name of a candidate contesting an election may sound familiar to a voter even if the voter may not be actually familiar with the contestant. That brand of television set or that person who appears familiar is more likely to be chosen.

The availability bias, also known as availability heuristic, is nothing but a mental shortcut, one that works on instant examples that strike a person's mind when he is in the process

---

[3] Gary Becker, *The Economic Approach to Human Behavior*, University of Chicago Press, 1978.

of making a choice or taking a decision. It works on the rather compelling, if not altogether accurate, premise that if something can be recalled quickly, it must be worth. Contrarily, if a product, a person or an incident cannot be easily remembered, it must be unimportant. In other words, that which is recent gains precedence for its easier recall value, while those in a more distant past become less important. Not only that, those which are easily recallable also become more credible.

It was in the late 1960s and early 1970s that Kahneman and Tversky began work on understanding heuristics and biases. Until then, the popular notion was that human beings were rational in their thoughts and actions, using algorithmic processes to arrive at decisions. The path-breaking research by the academicians had an impact on a variety of fields—education, law, medicine and political science among others.

This is what the two researchers found in their study: when participants were shown two visual structures and asked to pick the one that had more paths, the participants saw more paths in the structure that had the more obvious available paths. They had based their final estimation on a quick first impression of the problem. The participants were given a short amount of time to make the estimation. Thus, they based their estimates based on what was easily available.[4]

In another experiment, participants listened to lists of names containing either 19 famous women and 20 less famous men or 19 famous men and 20 less famous women. Some of them were asked to recall as many names as possible, whereas others

---

[4] Amos Tversky and Daniel Kahneman, 'Availability: A heuristic for judging frequency and probability', *Cognitive Psychology*, Vol. 5/2, 1973. https://doi.org/10.1016/0010-0285(73)90033-9

were asked to estimate whether male or female names were more frequent on the list. The names of the famous celebrities were recalled more frequently compared to those of the less famous celebrities. The majority of the participants judged, incorrectly, that the gender associated with more famous names had been presented more often than the gender associated with less famous names.

Vividness is a potent tool in framing opinions or arriving at conclusions or forming emotions. The more vividly described possibilities get more rooted in our minds than those that are not so dramatically explained. For instance, there is less possibility of dying by a snake bite than in a road accident. But the snake bite is what we fear more. We see a snake a distance away and jump out of its way, even try to hurt it or kill it. It does not matter that the snake is non-poisonous. On the other hand, we are callous in observing road safety rules even when our carelessness could endanger our lives.

This is because snake-bites have been vividly described in texts and shown on television. Snakes have featured in television shown attacking their prey. Things that are more conspicuous become more important to us. In a room full of people, our vivid memories would be of those people who are particularly well or ill-dressed; or those who indulge in dramatics when making their point. We will not easily remember those who are low-profile or soft in their approach.

The story does not become important but the way it is narrated, because the latter makes it more vivid. Stereotypes get created in the process. Take a vastly diverse country, such as the United States for instance, with so many different cultures and ways of life changing from state to state and even city to city. A man from Texas has a set opinion about a person from Los Angeles. Someone living in the industrial hub of New York may find difficulty relating to a resident in Tennessee who may be comparatively conservative and religious in terms of their way of life. This is because of the vividness with which one community has been taught about the other. Thanks to the difference in the histories of the Northern and Southern American States, the sprouting of cultural, linguistic and social differences is only natural. Whoever said America lacked culture or was homogenous in terms of its population?

Ideas that get imprinted in our memory, even without our knowing it, determine our opinions, biases and actions. Psychologists from an institution in Yale conducted an experiment. Two sets of students were given a bunch of words each to create grammatically correct sentences. The first set was given words that related to the elderly—slow, deliberate, careful. The second set had words that replaced elderly and were neutral. Once the task was done, all the students were asked to walk down the hallway, and their pace of walking was secretly measured.

Students who had created sentences with the words related to the elderly were measured to have walked slowly and deliberately, as compared to the other set of students who had used neutral words. Matters related to elderliness had got imprinted into the minds of those students so subtly that they did not realize it—but responded to it accordingly. If we are exposed to something—a photograph, a drawing, a suggestion, an idea or words as in the above case—we tend to develop some sort of an affection or relatability towards it.

Forget the old saying, 'Familiarity breeds contempt.' Here, familiarity breeds acceptance. What comes most easily to mind—the mental bias or the mental availability—becomes the truth. The terms 'familiar' and 'accurate' become synonymous.

The power of repetition is evident all around us, in different areas of activity. The advertising industry's survival depends on this concept. It launches a new soft drink by extolling its virtues. Then, it repeats those virtues throughout its campaign over and over again until they are ingrained in the minds of potential consumers as familiar and, therefore, true. That's how sales happen.

The political system uses the 'familiar and, therefore, true' trick to good effect. A political party sells itself to the voters by promising a host of sops, repeatedly. It also repeatedly reminds the voters of its position on important national issues. Over a period of time, what it says is taken to be believable and the party reaps the electoral rewards.

Celebrated boxer Mohammad Ali used this concept to his benefit. When he repeatedly said, 'I am the greatest,' he may have believed it. But the real target were his opponents. Hearing it again and again, they too must have been psychologically struck and began to believe that they stood no chance against him. After all, he was the greatest.

Another good example of the mental availability is that of the direct selling firm, Amway. It told customers that they could earn while they bought Amway products, which range from personal care to health supplements and others. The products were good, and the company saved on the expenses involved through the traditional selling route of wholesalers and retailers. It said that part of those savings was getting directed to the customers. Repeated hammering of the message worked and the organization's message and products began to come easily to mind.

Mental readiness is about opting for a product or service automatically, whereas not choosing it would need deliberation.

When one feels hungry while driving about, the first name that comes to mind is McDonald's. That is how the non-conscious, or the heuristic system, operates. We have to take a conscious decision to not opt for McDonalds.

There is another message here: because the fast-food outlet is so readily available, the mental readiness to pick it is greater. We may decide to lose weight and give up on potato chips and other junk food. But if that is the only thing readily available in our kitchen, it will be difficult to resist it. If the fridge is stocked with fresh fruit and protein cereals, it becomes that much easier for us to make a choice, because the mental readiness meets the availability of the desired product.

Research conducted across the globe demonstrated that people who have soft drinks and junk food readily available in their homes are overweight as compared to those that do not stock those products. On the other hand, those who had fruit and other healthy products in their homes were more healthy and fit. The trick, thus, is to control the visibility of the products and make our mental readiness tuned to the situation.

The theory can be applied at the workplace too. Take the case of two employees. One is more noticeable because of his good dress sense and a readiness to take on responsibilities. He is seen whenever there is a crisis situation that needs to be handled. His work table is neat and well organized. He is accessible to his colleagues. The other employee is low-key and remains in the background most of the time, not willing to take the lead. He is reticent and does not easily mix with others. Who would come easily to mind when the boss sits down for an evaluation? The first, naturally, who can expect a raise in salary. The second one may be as competent in his work, but he is likely to lose out because of poor visibility.

An organization's chief executive or the head of department has a tough task trying to match the salary of an employee with his performance. The employee understandably believes he deserves more, but what is more important is that his boss should believe similarly. It is rare for the boss to give a salary higher than what the employee suggests, and the employee thus gives an expectation on the higher side. The boss then adjusts it to a lower level, which could be what the subordinate had wanted.

This is also true of charitable firms approaching donors for help. They will set the bar high, because they know the donor will lower it to an amount that is smaller than what is sought.

In a room where everyone is seated for a meeting, the man who stands, stands out. In the classroom, the student who slinks in the back rows is not noticed by the teacher; the one who takes the front seat is visible. The front row student may not raise his hands or ask questions, but he still gets the attention. The student in the back may ask a few questions, but the teacher is likely to give little attention to him—perhaps presuming that the boy is merely seeking some attention.

It often happens that when you get a new idea, you are so excited that you wish to share it in detail with your colleagues or your boss. That is not a good approach. Begin by sharing only the bare essentials. Let the idea be absorbed, and let it be discussed to the level of it being workable or not. Make it familiar and obvious. Wait for a few days, and then expand upon it. The automatic system, which works on the 'familiar', will help you in your quest.

When people want to get rid of a bad habit or want their loved ones to quit such a habit, it helps to keep the matter visible. Notes pasted on the walls of the study or the bedroom, saying 'Thank you for quitting smoking,' or 'I can do it! I can quit smoking,' is a good idea.

It works also when you wish to adopt a good habit. 'I will eat fruits daily' or 'I will go for my walk daily, come rain or sunshine,' are some examples. You will be amazed how well these methods work. This is the power of mental availability—the power of the visible.

Most of us are familiar with how Apple ran a widespread campaign with the iconic catchphrase, 'If you don't have an iPhone, well, you don't have an iPhone.' It proved to be an instant hit. Why? Because the ads showed you what you were missing if you didn't yet own the iconic phone, and of course, because we were all so familiar with the ads on TV, social media, newspapers and magazines. One commercial showed a lightning fast app download on the app store, another praised iTunes and the built-in iPod on the phone and the third showed the wonders of iBooks. The ads appealed to the iPhone envy that some (including you, if you didn't own one) might have felt and also portrayed Apple phones as far superior, giving you the impression that if you wanted a really good phone, they were your *only* choice.

The salesman at a store selling laptops could begin by showing a potential customer the high-end laptops and judge the person's response. Accordingly, he can then guide him to the low-priced ones, because he will have realized that that is what the customer wants. The important thing is that the consumer's appetite for the product is aroused enough to make a purchase.

All this is not to say that responses to the automatic system always work. Blackberry, for instance, was a company that folded up over the years despite its innovative, visible ad campaign which most of us remember as the catchy 'We're the Blackberry boys' song that got stuck in our heads. But by and large, understanding the language of the automatic system works.

Association of Ideas

An idea that occurs to us does not come in isolation. It has an association of other ideas. Each of these triggers even more ideas. Hyundai gives us the idea of a car. Then comes the idea of a model. The price. The colour. The status involved in owning it. When you think of 'young', you have ideas of rippling muscles, an athlete, black shiny thick cap of hair and being tech-savvy. Each of these ideas contribute to creating a profile and help in persuading that person to perform or not perform an act.

Associations happen spontaneously; the mind cannot switch off its function. Memories, more memories, emotions of all kinds—they all flood our mind. This is not a conscious activity but non-conscious. And through them, we get to know ourselves better, realizing that we know so less that we thought we did.

We use these ideas that connect with the original to create a new explanation of our situation. Ideas that were not generated out of association (non-consciously) do not enter the narrative—nor do they influence the outcome.

Ideas can also be in the form of symbols or signs. Semioticians, who study the science and systems of communication, have done cutting-edge research on the subject in the recent decades. They have also reflected upon the differences between signs and symbols. If you see a 'no parking' sign alongside the road, associated ideas get triggered in your non-conscious mind: a car, a disregard of rules and the consequences (in the form of the vehicle being towed away or a fine that one has to pay on the spot or in court). The Statue of Unity in India or the

Statue of Liberty in the US are both symbols. They too have many associated ideas, but the association of ideas will differ with different people. You may not get the same answer from two people. That is because a symbol does not have a direct, explicit message—unlike a sign.

Symbols, unlike signs, do not have any explicit meaning. The understanding of symbols is through implicit associations. The Apple logo, or that of Twitter, conveys nothing—unless you associate it with quality and pathbreaking innovation in technology, or for the latter, with the power of social media. Symbols depend on associate ideas triggered by the automatic system to be meaningful. There are no rational thoughts that derive from the reflective system.

Associations need not be accurate. A soft drink company sells its product by claiming health benefits that may not always be true. A cigarette manufacturing firm markets its product as a macho symbol—which again would be far from the truth. The reflective mind may think so but the automatic system does not. That is why product and service sellers play on the automatic system.

For instance, in the US, there was a great deal of talk about ObamaCare. Again, it was an idea that comprised many layers of policies and programmes but could be identified with one single symbol—protection against high health bills.

Each of these ideas triggered many associations. A seedling can represent the right to life; an open door can be associated with transparency. Very often, such symbols are used in films to make a subtle statement. A mother, with a little child in her arms, sees violent commotion on the streets and shuts the windows of her house. It symbolizes her desire to keep her child protected from the chaos outside.

Of course, these messages can be conveyed in other different ways too. Therefore, the actual structure of the symbols is not that important. But the creator of those symbols—the persuader—attaches associations to the symbols, and that makes the symbols powerful and easy to recall. Symbols can have vague meanings for different people, but they become precise when they are laden with associations. On the other hand, signs are more exact and not so flexible. A 'no honking' sign is just that and so is the 'no smoking' sign.

Why does association occur? Because one idea gives rise to another and then another until we have a string of ideas—all germinating from that one original idea. For the persuader, the task is to enhance the associations that come with ideas and use them in a way that will shape the behaviour of the target in ways that the persuader desires.

Let's take the case of vibrant democracies. Free voting is inherent to the liveliness of a democracy and people have to be persuaded to vote in large numbers. How can that be achieved? There are, of course, political workers who go door to door asking people to visit the polling booths and cast their vote. Associated ideas can be made to work too. Voting can be linked to patriotism, to a need for change or to assert a free citizen's right to express his or her opinion. This could work at both individual and societal levels. A motivated individual, suitably persuaded, can persuade others in his neighbourhood or in his circle of friends and associates.

The cascading effect is a boon for the persuader. All he needs to do is to convince one person who, in turn, can help in altering the behaviour of many others in ways that the persuader wants. If a salesman can convince a customer to buy an LG OLED television, that customer could put in a good word about the product to his neighbour or friend and more sales could happen. If some people in a locality go out to vote, encouraged by the associated ideas that have been put forth, others too would be more inclined to do the same—though they may not always have the same reasons for voting.

Associated ideas can also be used in reverse: to convince somebody against a particular line of action. The son wants to buy a particular brand of motorcycle, but the father is not happy with the choice. Instead of directly refusing the choice, the father invokes the associated ideas with the brand that the son wants—machoism, speed, daring and reckless adventure. The son is a sober person and does not relate to any of them. He gets persuaded to drop the particular brand.

Creating a level of indecision works. But it is indecision that the marketer—the persuader—loathes. Indecision is destructive to his cause, which is why when one is promoting a brand or a cause, the message through signs or symbols is direct and decisive.

At times, associated ideas can present a company with an image that it wants but does not have, because the work it does today does not justify it. However, at some point in the near future, it aims to do that work. Since the present matters, it wants the image created today to leverage it for the future.

Take an example. An automobile company does not manufacture electric cars, but it wants to be known as energy-friendly. It asks its publicity department to create an image of energy-friendliness. The firm comes up with associated ideas. It creates a series of video campaigns where the company is shown to be developing electric cars for the near future. It has its senior personnel talking of green energy as the future of the company. The video shows a housing complex for its employees that has large green areas, trees and plants.

The motor firm is not a clean energy company today, though it hopes to be one someday in the future if it follows up on its plans. But by the power of association, it has become a clean-energy friendly company today.

We can use the power of association in other ways. A horse denotes energy; the horse that is shown to suddenly race out of a stable symbolizes the release of pent-up energy. A languidly moving lion in a jungle setting shows a supremely confident being who is in no hurry to prove its monarchy. A dog demonstrates loyalty. No wonder that several advertisements use animals to convey a message—through the power of associations.

Brand associations, if not handled carefully, can backfire as well. Spirit Airlines transported commuters from wherever they live to the shores of Florida. After the Florida coast was hit by a massive oil spill, tourists refused to fly there. The airlines—ramping up its operations to the Atlantic coast—began to advertise tongue-in-cheek: 'Check out the oil on our beaches.' It meant the sun tan oil, but the people were put-off by the 'too clever' half-message, which they associated with the oil spill. The advertisements may have been cleverly written, but they were ill-suited to the ground reality.

3

SPEAK THE STYLE

If the persuader knows the language of the target, that's good. But if he can also speak the language in the style that the target does, that would be great. As we have seen before, the language style would consist of emotion, action and particular likes and dislikes. They all emerge out of the automatic system and are accentuated by associations and availability—both of which enhance the mental availability or readiness.

Action is often confused with motivation. If a man climbs on to a high-powered motorcycle and drives off, it can be assumed that he is motivated by the need to reach a destination quickly. That is need, not motivation. Experienced persuaders pay closer attention to the action, not the motivation. An observer tends to judge an action, even if that action may have been the only choice the actor had. Take an example. The court is in session. The man stands in the dock; he is accused of rape. The court has assigned a lawyer to defend him. The lawyer feels strongly against rape and does not like rape accusations. But that does not matter to the observers who watch the proceedings of the court. Their opinions are coloured against the lawyer—how can a person defend a rape accused?

Social psychologists call it fundamental attribution error,

or FAE. It is also known as correspondence bias or attribution effect. The FAE is a tendency in people to under-emphasize the situational or environmental explanation for a person's behaviour in a said context. It is described as 'The tendency to believe that, what people do reflect who they are.' The phrase came into use after Lee Ross coined it, following an experiment conducted by two social scientists, Edward E. Jones and Victor Harris in 1967.[5]

The experiment was conducted on subjects who were asked to prepare essays for and against Fidel Castro. Then these same subjects were told to rate the attitudes of pro-Castro and anti-Castro writers. The pro-Castro writers were rated as being personally favourable towards the dictator. Even when they were told that the pro-Castro writers were told to write in that manner, their opinion remained the same. The subjects were unable to understand the situational aspect—that the situation had demanded from some writers to be pro-Castro and others to be anti-Castro.

Now, take a hypothetical case of an essay contest. One set of students wrote favourable pieces on Saddam Hussein. The other set wrote against him. A panel was asked to evaluate not the essays but the mindset of the essay writers. Invariably, those who wrote in favour of the dictator were thought of as problematic. The panellists were then told that the pro-Saddam writers had been specifically told to take a favourable position. But that did not change the opinion of the panel members.

---

[5]Edward E Jones and Victor A Harris, 'The attribution of attitudes', *Journal of Experimental Social Psychology*, Vol. 3/1, Pp. 1–24, 1967. https://doi.org/10.1016/0022-1031(67)90034-0

Action, Not Motive, Counts

Marketers and other persuaders very often use the FAE or the internal attitudes of a target—though they may not call it by that name.

Bata Corporation is best known for its shoes. It was founded originally in the Czech Republic and Slovakia dating back to before the Second World War. It has been a family-owned business, with a presence today in more than 70 countries. In recent years, Bata decided to have a change in its brand image. That was easier said than done. Bata was considered to be a staid, old company; solid, dependable—but not exciting, and certainly not fashionable. It had to become fashionable to attract the new generation. So far, the brand had done what it did, because it wanted to be seen as reliable, not flashy.

It was enough for Bata to one day declare that it wanted to be fashionable. But claiming to be fashionable does not work in the eyes of the customer. There are perceptions of the past that are involved, and those have to be changed. Action, not words, are needed. People judge a brand by action. It launched the #ComeAndBeSurprised campaign, inviting people to the Bata stores and see for themselves that changes were coming in its products and services. In India, for example, Bata roped in the new generation by using popular actors to promote the brand. Bata wanted to express that it was beyond the routine school shoes or the unimaginative executive shoes. That was new action with new associations.

There may be instances when a company is not what it presents itself to be. A coal mining firm issues advertisements to demonstrate its commitment to combat environmental pollution. It may not actually be environmentally conscious, but it can convince people that it is by launching campaigns to plant trees or promote clean drinking water or distribute air cleaning equipment at subsidized rates. It can donate money to NGOs involved in environmental issues. Action, not intent counts in the automatic system.

When the time comes for you to vote, you may choose a candidate that acts honest—even if a particular act of honesty is motivated and not really sincere. You would like a candidate who is transparent—even if a particular act of transparency was motivated by the desire to present an open-minded facade behind which actually lurks a rigid mindset. Act in a particular way, and that is how others perceive you. The motive doesn't matter.

Let's say the reader spots an advertisement in a newspaper that says, 'Live big, live happy', accompanied by a photograph of a man intimidating a woman. At the bottom of the advertisement, is the line, in smaller size: 'But not by being indecent'. The ad may be creative, but the casual reader will connect the photograph to the first, more prominently displayed line of action. The motive of the ad maker is irrelevant; the action matters.

A little child does not easily eat food. It has to be persuaded. Do the parents lecture the child on the nutritional merits of the food that it is being given? Of course not, because that would not work. So, the parents eat that food and show pleasure and relish. 'Oh, how tasty, yummy, yummy!' they exclaim. That action convinces the child to try it out. Or, even if it does not, it had a better chance than a speech on the nutritional aspect. The child does not question its parents' motivation in exclaiming that the foods is tasty and fun. It notices action and is convinced.

The same principle applies to other chores. Your daughter

may not like to cook or do work in the kitchen. You cannot persuade her by rational arguments. But if you do that work yourself and express pleasure, she may be convinced. I know of an elderly lady who used the broom and duster in her house with a song on her lips. She told her granddaughter that keeping the house clean pleased the Gods, because God disliked unclean homes and visited those that were kept clean. Removing cobwebs and dirt was like cleansing our mind of bad thoughts, she added. The granddaughter was persuaded. Maybe the elders believed in what they said, or maybe it was done with a motive. But the automatic system does not see motive, it sees only action.

One kind of action leads to reciprocity. If you smile at a stranger, it is more likely that the stranger will smile back at you. If you are accommodating with your colleague, then there will be reciprocity. You may have had a motive. You have been told that the stranger is an influential person and could be of use to you some day. You know that the colleague is close to your boss, and being in the co-worker's good books could fetch you a promotion. But that does not matter in the language of the automatic system and its style.

Such social exchanges are very different from economic dealings. You go to a shop, pay for your goods and walk away with the material. There is no sense of obligation at either end. Economic exchange works best when personal relations do not get involved. On the other hand, social exchanges are personal and meant to create relationships. I may invite a neighbour for dinner, but that invitation may be accepted months later. Nevertheless, a relationship gets built on the spot when the invitation is extended.

Where does this obligation to reciprocate come from? It is inherently built within our system. After a customer makes a sizeable purchase from a jewellery shop, it is likely that he will trade for a cup of tea by the owner of the shop. We know that the offer of the tea was motivated by the sales, but we are still impressed and delighted by the action. At time, even before the sales is done, tea or soft drinks is offered to a customer. This is again done with a motive—to tune the customer to purchase. The customer, although he knows it, is impressed by the action.

Sentiments Matter

The automatic system makes use of emotions to strike a communication and thus understands the language of emotions and responds readily to it. Love, happiness, fear, revulsion and various other emotions or sentiments form the language's style.

The effect of liking is what psychologists refer to as 'affect heuristic'. It is a sort of mental shortcut that helps people make decisions or quickly solve issues with the help of emotions. This is a subconscious or a non-conscious process that allows people to go through the process of decision-making without conducting an extensive research or study on the issue at hand. It is like a stimulus.

Take two examples. The word 'cancer' stimulates fear and dread, whereas 'mother' generates an emotion of unconditional love and longing. The research on the two subjects can wait; the feelings are instant. The 'affect heuristic' is used by persuaders even if they do not use that term. They understand that, in making choices, the target often goes by a gut feeling. If the gut feeling is positive, then it generates positive feelings. If it is negative, then negative thoughts dominate, where the risks are seen as high and benefits, low.

Health awareness campaigns often make use of the 'fear'

factor to attract the target's attention. An adequate level of anxiety is first created, and then a solution is provided. A study by Averbeck, Jones and Robertson (2011), looked at how prior knowledge influenced the response to fear.[6] Surveys were distributed which manipulated prior knowledge as low or high and two different topics: sleep deprivation or spinal meningitis.

Various scales were used to test how prior knowledge affected certain health-related issues. Researchers found that individuals who had earlier knowledge in a certain subject exhibited less fear and were less likely to fall prey to the affect heuristic. But individuals that did not have prior knowledge exhibited more fear.

An experiment was conducted by Schmitt and Blass (2008).[7] They produced two versions of an anti-smoking film. One contained high fear arousal and the other did not. Participants (46 non-smoking students and five smoking students) expressed stronger anti-smoking behaviour than when they viewed the low fear-arousal version.

Thus, our pre-existent sentiments, rather than an understanding that comes with details, dominate our immediate responses which the automatic system taps into. That is why our prejudices lead us to information that suits our bias. If one likes a particular film star or a politician, one picks and chooses

---

[6]Joshua M. Averbeck, Allison Jones and Kylie Robertson, 'Prior Knowledge and Health Messages: An Examination of Affect as Heuristics and Information as Systematic Processing for Fear Appeals', *Southern Communication Journal*, Vol. 76/1, 2011. https://doi.org/10.1080/10417940902951824

[7]Carol Schmitt and Thomas Blass, 'Fear appeals revisited: Testing a unique anti-smoking film', *Current Psychology: A Journal for Diverse Perspectives on Diverse Psychological Issues*, Vol. 27/2, Pp-145–151, 2008. https://doi.org/10.1007/s12144-008-9029-7

information and news which reflect that person in a good light. If, on the other hand, our emotions are negative, then we will highlight information that presents the person in a bad light.

Remember the Johnson & Johnson advertisements for baby care products? The baby smiles sweetly while the mother lovingly applies the talcum powder. What emotion does the ad send across? That the mother, for whom her baby is the most precious in the world, trusts J & J products. The persuasion is done. The immediate impact of the advertisement on mothers and would-be mothers would be to try out the product. An instant opinion has been formed by the automatic system.

Nearly every baby product does similar emotional advertisements, essentially speaking the language of the automatic system in a style that involves sentiments. Pampers is a good example. It is part of a giant global corporation with sales of upward of $80 billion. Both Pampers and J & J are probably genuinely concerned with a child's health. But even if that motive is limited to sales, the motive does not come in the way of the automatic system at work. The advertisements influence the perception of the target audience. When mothers visit a store for purchases, they would be automatically drawn to these products, thus enhancing the chance of their sales.

It helps if the target audience is 'rewarded' for making an emotional choice. If the man in the family quits smoking, a small celebration by the family to mark the feat can do wonders. Exchange vouchers and gift vouchers also perform a similar task. When a young man gives a rose to the woman he loves, the rose itself has no meaning except when it is seen as an emotional symbol of love and submission.

The persuader also has to reconcile the emotions he seeks to generate with the grounded truth. Despite the creative Onida

TV ad, the brand died out later because there was nothing left in it to 'envy'. Other brands had overtaken it in terms of performance and cutting-edge technology.

There are other ways when an emotional pull can fail to work—especially when there is too much aggression. Emotion and aggression do not go together. For instance, if an apparel brand were to advertise that those who don't patronize is still living in the cave age, it would be a case of going over the top. The message may have been well-meant and direct, but the association is that of negativity and can put off the target.

This is because people instantly respond to campaigns emotionally and not through reason. If reason were to be applied, they would appreciate the creativity involved and also the subtle messaging. But that is not the language or style of the automatic system.

Copycat Phenomenon

The non-conscious mental system also dips into the preferences of others to frame its own choice. If the majority in a room full of people raise their hands in affirmation when asked about the acceptability of a product, some, if not many, of those that did not raise their hands are likely to be influenced by the majority. The thought process would be: if so many people like the product, there must be something positive about it. Once that sentiment sets in, the automatic system does the rest.

Reebok is associated with sports. There will be people who are acquainted with the brand and the associations connected with the product. There will also be those who love it, though they may not possess it. And there will be others who are owners of Reebok products—sports shoes, sports apparel, etc. A large circle of lovers and owners of the product would indicate a greater acceptance of the positive values.

However, there are products that consciously advertise themselves as exclusives, not mass consumed. The idea is to create a niche group of owners and lovers, though the circle of acquaintances may be large. The emotion that is conveyed through these products is that they are not for everyone but only the discerning consumer who is willing to pay a possibly higher price for it. In the 1960s and 70s, not everybody owned a Rolls Royce. If they had, then the car would have lost its niche appeal. Not everybody today owns a Ferrari LaFerrari, which comes with a price tag of $1.4 million. The emotion here is one of exclusivity. Those who can afford it and decide to buy it are driven by their automatic system. They do not analyse whether the price is justified. Even if the same features are available in a lesser priced car, they opt for the expensive one.

But researchers have discovered one thing for a fact. That the more a product has friends (those who like it though they not have it), the more it has lovers (those who possess it). Nike scores over another brand because it has more friends, in certain countries. In others, it could be Reebok or some other brand.

Social scientist William McPhee had in 1963 discovered a phenomenon in which, barring very few exceptions, the lower market-share brand had both lower brand loyalty and fewer buyers over a period of time. He called this empirical law, 'Double Jeopardy'.[8] McPhee first observed the case in the awareness and liking ratings for Hollywood actors. He later found it in readers of comic strips and listeners of radio jockeys.

---

[8]William McPhee, *Formal Theories of Mass Behavior*, Free Press, 1963.

It was not long after that another social scientist Andrew Ehrenberg discovered that the Double Jeopardy law applied to brand purchases. Today, it is seen to apply across categories, as diverse as detergent to aviation fuel, all over the world. For the persuader, the phenomenon is critical to understanding the behavioural patterns of his target consumer. It shows that the growth of a brand's market share depends, to a large extent, on the size of a brand's customer base. If that does not happen, increasing the brand's market penetration becomes a herculean, often impossible, task.

Of course, in seeking to increase brand penetration and base, the persuader must take care not to compromise with the distinctiveness of the brand. As we discussed earlier, some brands often deliberately keep a low penetration level in order to safeguard their niche appeal. Brands succeed when they appeal emotively to their target audience and promise to deliver on them. Those who want the feel of an athlete would come to, say Nike or Reebok. If these brands were to dilute their image of being 'athlete-friendly', they would be seen as betraying their customer expectations and face the consequences.

Retail companies, such as Gap, have long emphasized value and quality over price in their marketing strategies. Gap's 'Dress Normal' campaign got it right. Former Gap global CMO Seth Farbman appropriately summed up the company's mindset, explaining, 'What we need to reinforce is what has always been true, that even at full price, the quality and value and enduring style of Gap product is of high value.' Honda, too, transformed its brand image in the 1970s and 1980s by focusing on building high quality cars with the right features at the right price for its core target. Today, Honda is seen not as 'cheap' but as a smart purchase.

The ability of others to influence our behaviour through their behaviours is best amplified in community exercises. Yoga has caught on to the world today. There are laughing sessions, where a group of people gather and stimulate laughing sessions. This is not done through humour or the cracking of jokes. It is just pure laughter for the sake of laughing and is considered a good exercise to unwind and relax the nerves. Someone, who is a newcomer to the session and would otherwise feel uncomfortable laughing just like that, catches on the mood too and laughs in an inhibited manner. The laugher of others makes us laugh too, even when we are fully aware that the laugh is stimulated and without any apparent purpose.

Why does this happen? It is because we are pre-programmed to imitate—or be influenced by imitation. Our social behaviours are shaped by such pre-programming. When a person seated next to the driver in a vehicle yawn, it can stimulate a similar sense of boredom in the driver, which is why one is careful not to yawn when seated next to the driver. In the company of elderly people who move slowly, even a young man non-consciously adjusts his pace accordingly.

When an elderly person is in the company of children, he tries to be in the hop-skip-jump mode. When people are moving about at a furious speed in a busy street, even the lingering person adopts a pace to merge with the environment.

Such a behaviour is not consciously driven. We don't tell ourselves, 'Imitate those around you.' It is the automatic system at work. When one visits a new city or a new country, one non-consciously observes and behaves like the other people there. But while we imitate, there must be some reason for that. We let others guide our choices because we believe that the choice of others—when so many of them make it—has to be correct, or at least worth considering.

It is what behavioural scientists call the 'information cascade'. A number of people make the same decision in a sequential manner, one guided by the other through the automatic system. The information cascade works as follows:

1. A decision had to be made (whether to eat in a new restaurant, for example).
2. The choice is binary: yes or no.
3. People make the decision sequentially, and each person gets to observe the other's reaction.
4. Each person has some information apart from their own that guides the decision.
5. While a person does not know what information the other has, he makes inferences about the information from how that person behaves with regards to the choice.

The Cascading Effect

Amazon has orange coloured star ratings for the products it sells. A rating of four or more persuades the potential customer to try out the product. He does not know much about its virtues but is guided by the ratings given by others. It does not matter that a lower rating given to a product may not actually complement its real value. The same is true of trip advisor sites that rate hotels and places of tourist interest and of music web sites.

The cascading effect works in yet another way. The early responder in a group impacts the thoughts of others. Take a meeting of a union of workers. The first worker to speak sets the tone for the others. He may raise issues of low pay, management bias, poor work conditions, etc. The ones who speak thereafter would take their cue from the issues raised by the first speaker. This will happen if the second speaker raises other matters as well—those fresh subjects will determine the thoughts and minds of the others to follow.

Seated in the front row, if you rise to applaud the speech of a person, the others in the crowd will soon join you in the act. Conversely, if you decide to question some of the arguments made by the speaker, there is more likelihood of some others backing you up. The first speakers are, therefore, persuaders who have used the automatic system's language and style to craft the responses of others. Not many of the later responders would have thought in-depth about the assertions of earlier speakers, and yet, they would have been bought into the arguments.

We often hear of present-day actors talking of the influence early generation actors had on them. This is not just polite talk but the cascading effect at work. If an earlier actor projected a role in a particular way, some aspects of that projection seeps into a later actor's portrayal of a similar character. In fact, a few of the legends of acting are referred to as 'schools of acting' within themselves.

There is a lesson in this act of imitation. If you want to influence the behaviour of others, then do what you want them to do. If you identify a veteran by name in a room full of military men and praise him for the services he has rendered, others will also do the same. You offer a seat in a crowded bus to a needy person, and the probability of others to repeat the gallant act increases.

Take another example. There are only a few pieces of a particular jewellery left in a showroom; the rest have been sold out. You will quickly want to purchase it. You do this not *per se* because there is only limited stock available—that is not the motivation—but because others have bought it in such large numbers that only a limited stock is left. What is scarce becomes even more attractive.

Advertisers, who are essentially persuaders, understand the power of the cascading effect. Thus, a product is advertised as 'America's favourite', 'The number one choice of France' or one that 'Millions across the world trust'. There may be no way of knowing if that is indeed the case, but the lines speak the language of the automatic system and in a style that appeals to the emotive mind.

The trick works with children—and even more forcefully. If in a residential, a number of kids are seen using skate-rollers, other children would also pester their parents to own a skate-roller. If many in a group of friends has watched the film, *Django Unchained*, the others would be eager to view it as well.

If the preference of others in the present has a cascading impact, creating an impression that it would be the preference of most in the immediate future can work wonders for the persuader. A cloth detergent product can promise to remove all obstinate stains, a shoe can promise to elevate your level of athleticism, a shirt can promise to give you that extra edge in an interview, or a deodorant can promise to make you the centre of attraction in a meeting. The persuader has to understand the wishes of the people and then promise to fulfil them.

It is hard to go against popular notion, unless one wants to be a lone wolf. True, the lone wolf has his own charm, but for all the attraction that it holds, few people would want to be lone wolves. The advertiser has to create a notion of popularity to attract consumers. Popularity comes often after popularity is claimed. Legendary boxer Mohammad Ali would say, 'I am the best.' even before he became the undisputed king of the boxing ring.

But what determines popular notion? Finding that is not as easy as it sounds. Take the example of a supermarket. Its advertisers conducted an exercise among customers and non-customers in the vicinity of the mart to explore what they expected from the store. A section said they hoped for low prices, others placed emphasis on customer service. Still others said they would expect all their daily needs to be met and would be disappointed if the store failed to meet those needs and they had to go elsewhere for the items. Some of the respondents wanted a cheerful environment—good lighting, products exhibited attractively on the shelves, a nice wall paint. Each segment of the respondents had different demands and expectations.

The differing desires actually took the attention off from the essentials—that is, good quality products at a reasonable price. A small neighbourhood store could give what the expansive supermarket could not. If the advertisers were to get caught in the differing demands of respondents, they would be unable to craft an advertising strategy that worked. They needed to concentrate on a single point of strength that made the superstore different from its competitors. Otherwise, they will end up convincing one segment but not the rest. If one segment emphasizes on price, the other may be put off by that emphasis, because in their view, low price would mean a compromise with quality. If one segment talks of cheerful interiors, the other segment would see it as a distraction from what they may perceive as poor-quality products or services.

Such a conflict is evident in our day-to-day life. If an elderly person does something, the younger generation will view it as not modern and refrain from imitating. If the young son insists on wearing earrings, the mother will see it as a form of defiance and resist. The persuader must realize that these different segments may appear to be in conflict, but they are not enemies of one another. They are only a little different from one another, and the difference can be reconciled through smart marketing ways that use the automatic system's language and style.

An established car manufacture may have several high-selling models. But then, it makes a model that does not catch the public imagination and is shelved after a year or so. The marketer made the mistake of assuming that since the manufacture's reputation is already well-established, anything that it offers will be accepted. It failed to factor in the emotive demands of the consumer. One segment of consumers may have found the shape of the car odd; another segment could have concluded that the new model was not very different from the earlier one and yet more expensive.

The above instance is one of making a product readily available and yet, not getting the full advantage of that availability; unlike, say, in a home fridge which stocks nutritious food items. The availability of healthy food propels a person to take it, unlike in the case where the lack of availability makes him choose unhealthy stuff which he is fond of. Talking to such a person about the health details of the food item will not work—the availability is more likely to have an impact.

If we can link healthy food with associate ideas such as fun and taste, there is greater likelihood of its acceptance, especially among children and the youth. For the elderly, the associated ideas would be freedom from niggling health issues. It is all about communication in a language and style that the automatic system understands. If the communication is dull and boring, the effect will be negative. Celebrities endorsing healthy food helps consumers make the right choice. On the other hand, if public figures promote stuff like cigarettes or alcohol, that can have a deleterious impact on the automatic system of the consumer.

The reflective system is often subordinate to the automatic system, but there are times when it comes into action and seeks to readjust the automatic system's responses. We may want to tell a person to 'go to hell', but the reflective system may persuade us to see reason. If celebrities endorse non-healthy products, our reflective system can, at times, see through the game and develop a dislike for the celebrities' action. Nonetheless, unlike the reflective system, our automatic system never goes to sleep or gets inactive, which is why it remains the predominant factor in our decision-making, which is often impulsive.

Obesity is a major problem that troubles many countries, from developed ones such as the US to developing ones such as India. Various campaigns have been launched by the government authorities in both countries to promote healthy eating habits. And yet, there has been little impact of these efforts. People continue to splurge on burgers, potato chips and ice-creams. One reason is that makers of such products are more adept at appealing to the automatic system of the customer. Besides, the easy availability of these products, delivered at one's doorsteps within minutes, adds to their popularity.

Promotional campaigns for healthy food have presumed that the rational mind will grasp their message. But the rational mind, or the reflective system, has to grapple with the automatic system's language and style, and it usually comes out as the loser. The solution is for advertisers of healthy food products to speak the language and use the style of the automatic system. Appeal to emotions through associated ideas.

Various market researchers have stated that decades of

wrong models of marketing have ruined many good products. Paul Feldwick wrote in *The International Journal of Market Research* that emotional tugs are stronger than rational pushes, and advertisers and product manufacturers have to come to terms with that reality.[9] Recent psychological and neuroscience research have amply indicated that the automatic system is the predominant trigger of consumer choice, and unless the advertisers recognize this reality, they will continue to plunder.

Perhaps one reason why the advertising industry has stuck to the old model is because it finds it easier to measure the reflective way of functioning. Rational choices are, after all, based on hard facts. In the choice of a car, the price can be measured, the engine power can be quantified, the seating capacity can be given a number and the fuel efficiency can be determined. On the other hand, automatic choices work on an emotive output which is difficult to measure. What is the point in showing light in the dark to a man who is not looking for something that he has lost but simply wants to be left alone? Conversely, a man drops his wallet in the street and looks for it under a lamppost, not because he may have dropped it there, but because there is light.

Even our romantic relationships or marriages, contrary to belief, are not based on rational choices. The two individuals do not evaluate their receptive partner's looks, pay-checks, skin colour or religion. If love has to happen, it just happens. It is the automatic system at work. A rational evaluation is often done by the families of the two individuals, and their effort generally goes to waste.

---

[9]Robert Heath and Paul Feldwick, 'Fifty Years Using the Wrong Model of Advertising', *International Journal of Market Research,* Vol. 50/1, January 2008. https://doi.org/10.1177/147078530805000105

These are realities. And yet, the advertising industry across the world has taken decades to understand it. It has been believed that rational choices can be engineered through smart marketing and punch lines. According to a study conducted by scientist Benjamin Libet and his team, we have an unconscious impulse to act about 500 milliseconds before acting, whereas we 'consciously' decide to act about 200 milliseconds before acting. In other words, the unconscious, or non-conscious impulse, which is part of the automatic system, causes both the decision and the act to happen.

Most often, we experience a thought that is followed by action. The assumption is that the thought triggered the action. But it wasn't the thought (which was conscious), but the non-conscious mind that made us act. And, when decisions are not made rationally, they are difficult to reverse. For example, if a consumer decides on a car with a good mileage, he is likely to change his choice if another car provides a better fuel efficiency. However, if a consumer decides non-consciously on a product, he is unlikely to change his mind.

4

TARGET THE ATTITUDE

It has become clear over the years that persuaders will bite the dust if they are engaged in changing the attitude of a person. It could be his attitude towards smoking, towards a political party, towards a particular brand of television, towards an economic ideology or even towards mercy killing. The failure is simply because the wrong target was chosen.

The persuader must, instead, concentrate on changing the behaviour of the person. Behaviour is action; and action is generally generated by the automatic system. The persuader succeeds if he can make a person give up smoking. The fact that the person's attitude towards smoking does not change is irrelevant. A voter may have a hostile attitude towards a political party, but if he is persuaded to vote for that party without a change in that attitude or behaviour, that is good enough.

On the other hand, you may be able to convince a person to change his attitude towards a politician from negative to positive. But the voter may still not vote for that politician, and the persuader will have failed his task.

Metropolitan cities are generally overcrowded and various government authorities are forever engaged in promotional campaigns—exhorting people to use public transport and avoid their own cars—to tackle traffic snarls on the roads. The advertising campaigns appeal to the good sense of the citizen, his responsibility towards others, towards reducing carbon emissions, improving the quality of air they breathe and towards reducing the risk of road rages and accidents. These campaigns seek to bring about a change in the attitudes of the commuter. Not surprisingly, they fail to work.

On the other hand, if parking fees are increased by a big amount, the efficiency of the mass transit system is improved, public buses are cleaner and function on time. There is ready availability of the public transport system in general; people are more likely to change their behaviour, even if their attitudes have not changed.

If a person's attitude also changes along with a change in action, that is a bonus. The reason why the persuader may not hesitate to change the attitude of a person is because he feels empowered that he has managed to alter a person's view on a particular subject. He feels a special kind of pleasure in making someone to agree to your world view. But in wanting to do so, he may miss out on the fundamental goal—to change the action of a person.

A marketer needs to make a person act the way he wants that action—changing his opinion or attitude is not important. But if the persuader still persists, it is because he finds it hard to believe that a person's change in action can happen without a change in attitude. But recent studies have indicated that the connection between attitudes and behaviours are tenuous.

Allan Wicker, a social psychologist, published a review paper in 1969 on the relationship between verbal expressions of attitude and apparent behaviours.[10] It led to a great amount of debate among experts and social scientists. In a series of studies that he conducted, he found no clear relationship between attitudes and behaviours. Job attitudes and job behaviours were not connected; attitudes and behaviours towards minority groups were different. Even attitudes and action on things like spending money or attending union meetings were non-connected. Later researchers expanded his findings. One found no relation between one's attitude towards cheating and actual cheating (action).

There have been some recent attempts to debunk this theory. Some experts have insisted that when attitudes are specific and not general, there is a connection. Attitude towards a minority group is general, but attitude over renting your premises to a minority member is specific. With a specific attitude, the action is relatable, they argue.

However, there is a caveat here. Specific attitudes are not what we understand as 'attitudes'. An attitude has to be general in order to determine a behaviour. Also, attitudes are hard to change, which is why it is better to try changing the action. If one takes the specific attitude of a person toward renting his premises to a member of a minority group, it could differ. He may rent the place if he knows the minority member and not rent it if he doesn't. Canadian author, social activist and filmmaker Naomi Klein, who leans to the Left, once remarked that 'intellectual antibodies' help us to keep our preconceptions alive. These antibodies are biases that constitute our attitudes towards various subjects. They are not easily changed.

---

[10]Alan Wicker, 'Attitudes versus Actions: The Relationship of Verbal and Overt Behavioral Responses to Attitude Objects', *Journal of Social Issues,* Vol. 25/4, Pp-41-78, 1969. https://doi.org/10.1111/j.1540-4560.1969.tb00619.x

The preconceptions can happen for a variety of reasons. The environment we live in, the people we interact with, the television programmes we watch and a host of other reasons. If we are exposed to a liberal environment, we develop liberal attitudes. If we watch a particular TV channel that espouses conservative values, our attitudes are shaped by that. The people who watch Fox News will have very different attitudes from those who watch the BBC News, as you might have already noticed in your conversations with relatives and friends during, for instance, Thanksgiving lunches or even birthday parties.

Take the Easy Way

There is no need to lose heart or fret. Take the surer way out by understanding that it's easier to change an act than an attitude. An act or behaviour can change with a change in circumstance, even if the attitude remains the same as before.

But attitude, along with circumstance, does play a role in the way people act. Except that the contribution is far smaller than that of circumstances. Attitudes are hard and inflexible whereas acts are malleable and can be managed with a change in circumstance or through emotive appeals. Change the circumstance and you can change the act of a person.

As a persuader, whether at home or at your workplace, you will desire that a person makes certain changes in his act; changes that you have been targeting at. Change the circumstance and side-step the intellectual antibodies that encourage resistance to change.

A customer walks into an ice cream parlour with his wife, with an intention to pick their favourite butter-scotch flavour. He finds that there is an offer of buy-one-get-one-free for the vanilla flavour. His attitude towards butter-scotch has not changed, but the circumstance has changed in the form of an attractive offer. It could very likely make him choose vanilla, though his favourable attitude towards butter-scotch has not changed.

Anne loves to shop at Walmart. Only recently, an outlet of Target has come up right outside the gates of her housing society. The circumstance has changed with the proximity of another supermarket to her home. She is very likely to visit the new store and even make purchases.

I may prefer a high-end iPhone to a Samsung smartphone. But when I enter a shop, I am told that Samsung is offering a $54 Sony headset free with the purchase of a particular series of its phone. I would consider buying a Samsung phone because of the changed circumstance, although my attitude towards the iPhone has not changed.

The trick, therefore, is for the persuader to change the circumstances to get the desired act. It would help for him to know that many social psychologists believe that as much as 99 per cent of our act is entirely driven by the automatic system.

The persuader must not think: what should I do to change people's minds? If he does that, he would be wanting to change somebody's attitude, and attitudes are hard, sometimes impossible, to change. Instead, he should consider: what can I do to make the person act the way I want him to?

We have considered above a few individual examples. But the technique can be applied to groups of people and even to organizations—whether government or private. Changing circumstance can help people make better decisions. An added achievement would be if the change in circumstances also brings about a change in attitude.

Tantalizing Connection

Thus, a change in behaviour can bring about a change in attitude. If we can make people act differently, it is possible that we can change how he feels. But does attitude cause behaviour, or does behaviour lead to a change in attitude? Research suggests that if you behave (or act) in a way that is inconsistent with your attitude, there are good chances of the attitude adjusting to the new act or behaviour.

The non-conscious system does not enjoy a dichotomy though the reflective thrives on evaluating the pros and cons. If you undertake an act that you have been persuaded to, you will over time, if not immediately, change your attitude to adjust your action or behaviour.

Social scientists and psychologists have studied people whose attitudes were inconsistent with their behaviours. They have subjects of their study to undergo acts that were not in consonance with their attitudes. For example, a group of people who were strong followers of a free, democratic system, were asked to write essays on the benefits of a dictatorial regime. Another group, consisting of pure vegetarians, was told to speak on the advantages of a non-vegetarian diet.

The first set not only presented arguments that demonstrated merits in a strong-handed regime but also underwent an attitudinal change to suit the positions they had just taken. In other words, they actually believed in what they wrote.

The second group of people, similarly, discovered the benefits of a diet of meat, detailing the greater availability of proteins and vitamins in a non-vegetarian diet. Because this was inconsistent with their attitude, they brought about a revision in the attitude as well to obliterate the duality.

Let alone stated positions, even when one is indifferent to a particular thing, one can be made to opt for a clear behaviour—which then results in a change in attitude. I may not have a particular position, positive or negative, on a Hitachi air-conditioner. But after I purchase it, I develop a positive attitude towards it. I had given the choice of another air-conditioner brand at the shop, a brand that I was again indifferent to. Had I chosen that brand, I would have most probably developed a similar positive attitude towards it and a negative one to the brand I had not purchased.

This is how the theories of cognitive consistency work. These theories have the principles of Gestalt psychology. Also referred to as 'Gestaltism', it is a theory of perception that emerged in the early twentieth century in Austria and Germany. In simple terms, it means that people perceive the environment in ways that are coherent and do not battle with their behaviours.

Cognitive consistency theories have their origins in researches conducted in 1993. At the heart is the assumption that people are motivated to seek simple attitudes, thoughts, beliefs, values and behaviours. If these are inconsistent, they will result in tensions and dilemmas, and propel an individual to simplify the situation by bringing about a match between the act they have done and their attitude.

If our attitude can change with a change in our act, and if our behaviour influences our attitude, then are we a product of our acts alone? A mismatch between the two does lead one to wonder, 'Who are we?' When we go according to our action, we reinterpret our attitude and reinterpret even who we are. In the end, we don't really know who we are, and that is precisely what the self-perception theory tells us. We may be strangers to those who don't know us, but we are also strangers to ourselves since we don't know who we are! We discover through our changed attitude that we are not what we earlier thought about ourselves.

Self-perception plays a big, even decisive, role in the choices we make. A person is born to a religion, and it's not his choice. He takes his religion as a given, because his parents have the same religion, and their parents had the same religion too. He does not sit down and objectively analyse various religions for their pluses and minuses.

If the parents are Buddhists and pray in a Buddhist temple, their children do the same. If the parents are Roman Catholics, their children attend Mass in the church. If the parents are Muslims, going to a mosque comes naturally to their children. And so on. These are all religious actions.

Let's suppose that a person, influenced by a preacher, decides to revisit his religion. He announces that he wishes to covert to another faith. His act of conversion may not be consistent with the attitude that he has developed over the years. An attitude that has been inculcated through his original faith. There will be a clash, and he will have to alter his attitude to tune it with his act, because he cannot take the conflict.

The theory of self-perception or cognitive consistency can be used in psychotherapy. A psychotherapist has to treat a patient with a problematic attitude. Since the doctor knows better than most that a change in attitude in solitude is next to impossible, he works towards persuading the patient to change his act, his behaviour, because that is an easier task. The hope is that, if the behaviour undergoes a change, the patient will change his attitude as well. As we have seen before, the conflict between a changed act and an unchanged attitude has to be resolved.

A patient walks into a psychotherapist's office, with a record of violent outbursts. He resorts to physical intimation at the smallest provocation, and wants to get out of the habit. The psychotherapist makes him join a community service centre, where the patient interacts with inmates who need attention, care and love. He observes other volunteers at work and sees the happiness that they derive in giving happiness to others. His behaviour undergoes a change as he also acts similarly. Over time, his attitude changes too, and he can be reformed.

The best way to change behaviours and attitude, thereafter, is to allow people do that by themselves, without making it seem that they are being led or coerced by others to change. In a community service, this is what exactly happens. If you bring a chain smoker in the company of men who are in advanced stages of cancer because of chain smoking, the fear of a similar thing happening to them can lead to a change in behaviour. Of course, this may not always work in some cases. Rapists and murderers are unlikely to reform if they are faced with victims of such crimes and the destruction of families that have been dealt.

The process of change in behaviour allows people to re-evaluate themselves for what they are and what they should be. When a man wears a military uniform, he is changed. The uniform stands for pride, duty, sacrifice and nationalistic feelings. The school uniform gives a student a sense of identity, a sense of purpose and a meaning in life. When a doctor wears his gown before undertaking an operation, he is internally preparing himself for the enormous responsibility that rests on his shoulders—saving the life of his patient.

It is not easy for parents to be persuaded to allow their children be inoculated in a mass inoculation drive conducted by their school, because they have many apprehensions. That is the attitude. But change the circumstance, and their behaviour can change, if not the attitude. The school can declare that children who get vaccinated will get an additional ten marks in the final examinations, they will get half a day off, or they can even skip a class for the next week.

Cognitive conflicts—the contrasts that arise from a change in behaviour with the attitude remaining unchanged—have become a subject of extensive study in recent years. The body-to-mind connection offers fascinating revelations for the expert. One can be assured that research being conducted will, in time to come, reveal even more secrets and unknown facts.

Already, some indications are available. If you step out of your home dressed particularly well, there is a perceptible change in your body language. You walk confidently, you exhibit a sense of determination, of purpose and you speak with authority. If you are shabbily dressed, you will walk loose-limbed, uninterestedly. There are exceptions: those in authority can dress anyway and still exude power. But exceptions don't determine the rule.

Even a small change can work wonders. Look at how a person changes his or her expression when taking a selfie. The selfie clicking is just half-a-minute exercise, but the change is dramatic. According to experts, this is because in that show time, the body suddenly produces more testosterone and less hormones that generate stress. By dressing like a powerhouse, a person can feel the power in himself. Low power, and possibly low self-esteem, happens when a person steps out poorly dressed.

The body-to-mind connection is evident in other ways too. When you perform a task that seemed difficult or even impossible initially, your mind tells you that you are an achiever, and your confidence soars to a level that you are prepared to take on even bigger challenges. On the other hand, if you fail to meet a challenge, you slump into self-doubt, and even otherwise simpler tasks look difficult.

When a person says to himself that he can 'do it', he is actually 'claiming' or 'pretending' to be up to the task. Because, unless he actually likes that job, he cannot be said to have had that ability. It is, therefore, important that one pretends with care. The wrong pretensions can have bad consequences.

Consider a college-going student. He has fed himself an overdose of superman stunts, having seen one film too many of that kind. He has seen the hero—wearing earrings and tattooed all over—make mincemeat of his adversaries, while mouthing abuses. The student now decides to pretend to be one of the hero's variety, and so he imitates his hero by getting tattooed and wearing rings in his ears and cultivating an abusive tongue. The pretension will not take him on the right path. The college student has defined himself in a certain way. His behaviour changes, and the danger is that his attitude too might change, for the worse.

The act of pretending can work in positive ways also. A celebrity is known for his involvement in charitable work. The school boy, who considers the celebrity his hero, can take up some work part-time with a charitable organization, say, an NGO that teaches slum children. He pretends to be a charitable person, and his attitude also changes as he gets more deeply involved with teaching the slum-dwelling children.

The persuader's task is to make people say they will do something, or say that they would not do something. It might sound on the surface that saying is not the same as doing. However, the chances of a person doing what he has committed himself to are greater than that of a person who had not committed himself.

A bunch of politicians want a leader to take on additional responsibilities, perhaps even become the head of their party.

The leader is reluctant, and the first challenge is to make him commit. As a fundamental question: do you want to get into active politics or not? Since the leader has already involved himself in a small way, he cannot possibly say no. Once an affirmation comes, the task of persuading him to act in the way that the group wants becomes easier.

Volunteers who commit themselves to do some work for an NGO are more likely to opt for it when an opportunity comes in the future than those who had been ambiguous. It is possible, though, that a change in circumstances can solicit a readiness from the fence-sitters. The change in circumstance could be a certificate of appreciation or even a token cash reward.

The above examples establish the power of commitment. If you want to persuade your co-worker, a family member, a friend or a customer, get that commitment from them. A commitment is that first step to bringing about an act that you desire from your target individual or group. It's like getting a foot in the door, a small step that people are more likely to take than a big one straightaway.

If a cab driver agrees to have a sticker on the windscreen of his car proclaiming, 'I respect people of all colours,' he has made a commitment. He would be more likely to be respectful towards customers of colour. If a person has a poster that says, 'I hate smoking,' he will contain his smoking habit, because he made a commitment.

This works rather well when you are seeking to persuade a group of people into a particular form of action. There are intermittent power supply failures in your housing society. If you ask residents to storm the power station and lock up the staff, few would be ready to join you. However, if you ask them to sign a petition that demands better service—failure of which will lead to a protest march to the electrical engineer incharge's office—many would comply. Because the commitment sought is small and is easily acceptable.

Commitment can change behaviour, and through behaviour, the attitude can change. People who otherwise had a nonchalant attitude towards power cuts would now alter their laid-back attitude as well.

Methods To Change the Act

If a persuader adopts the aim to change an act, he has, at his disposal, many ways to do so. This is always advantageous, for it offers him an array of choices; if one does not work, another can be applied. If one runs into the intellectual antibodies' shield, the persuader can deftly use another. In his basket, there will be at least one way that will change the target's behaviour, if not attitude.

You can make a consumer change his behaviour towards a product by changing its price, changing the packaging, changing its place of availability, tweaking the 'special' offers on it, changing its advertising pitch, and so on. One of these would surely change the consumer's act and possibly change his attitude in addition.

A grassroots political campaigner visits a locality where the attitude of the voters in general is antagonistic towards his party's candidate. He may find it difficult to change this attitude. But if he is able to guide the voters to places where he does not have to stand in a long queue, he is able to identify the many voters who are favourably disposed to his candidate, or he can help the voter with his voting card and voter's slip. He may be able to change the voter's behaviour in his favour without changing the voter's attitude.

There may be voters leaning towards a particular candidate, and the grassroots helper of that candidate's party can help ensure that they vote in large numbers. The helper can encourage them to vote early and thus lock up precious votes in his candidate's favour. Those who haven't voted yet need to be provoked to do so before the voting ceases. This can be done by raising various spectacles—their votes could make a difference between victory and defeat for their choice of a leader; and voting would demonstrate that they are stakeholders in a free and democratic system. The trick is to change the behaviour in favour of your candidate, not to attempt changing the voter's attitude—more so at the last moment.

Apple has done a good job at trying to change the act of customers without spending energy in changing attitudes. The computers have options to run programmes of Microsoft. Apple did not ask customers to change their attitude towards MS software and patronize its own. Instead, it changed the circumstance by offering MS options and targeted the behaviour of customers who chose Apple, although their attitudes towards MS remained unchanged.

Certain manufacturers do not ask consumers to switch over to their products. Instead, they offer incentives to consumers who 'try out' their products. 'Trying out' is the initial act and not the final one, which would be a more permanent migration of the customer from another product to their own. Some manufacturers even promise customers that, if they did not like the product, their amount would be refunded in full.

When you visit a shop to purchase a perfume, the sales executive sprays samples of different perfumes and asks you to choose. You smell the perfume—that is an initial act. The salesman does not ask you to buy any one of them. That is your decision, but the initial act of making you smell has been done.

The usefulness of an initial or intermediate act lies in the fact that it can lead to a final act which the persuader wants.

Visualize the Steps

An intermediate act could be more than one, leading to the final act. The persuader has to clearly think out the steps involved. What does a potential customer do before he decides on a high-end television set?

- He makes a short-list of the brands in the particular category.
- He checks on the price of each of those brands.
- He studies the features through brochures and on websites that compare various brands.
- He seeks advice from friends, family and acquaintances.
- He goes to the shop.
- He sees a demonstration of the product.
- If he is satisfied, he negotiates the best price he can get.
- He makes a purchase.

The sales executive must know these steps and be prepared. A customer walks into a car showroom and enquires about various brands and models. But to help him take the final step of making a purchase, the sales executive has to persuade him to undertake an intermediary act—a test drive. He can do that by telling the customer that he should get a feel of the drive before taking a decision. He can disarm the customer by stating that he does not want to make a sales pitch unless the customer is satisfied with his test drive experience.

Even seemingly small decisions are often arrived at through an intermediary act or a series of intermediary acts. If we want our family members to eat more apples than ice cream at home, we can work out a series of steps in that direction. Have apples always available in the fridge or in a fruit bowl on the dinner table for everyone to see. Make ice cream scarce in the freezer compartment of the refrigerator; put up posters extolling the nutritious virtues of the fruit.

These steps are more likely to work than just a monologue directed to the family on the need to eat more apples. It is easier to persuade people to keep apples on the dinner table rather than have ice cream. With a change in circumstance, the choice becomes easier, and the persuader gets the target to act as he wants.

The sales manager of a super store keeps a sharp eye on the preferences of his customers. Do they prefer plain potato chips to salted ones? Do they choose a particular brand of cornflakes over another? Depending on the choice, the display and availability of the more patronized products can be enhanced.

On the other hand, the sales manager can change circumstances to persuade people to make a particular purchase. Suppose that he wants his customers to adopt a healthy eating habit. He can reshuffle the products on the shelves in such a way that the healthier products are more prominently displayed while the others are pushed into the background. He can put up promotional posters alongside that informs about the nutritional values of the products he wants the customers to buy.

'This *instead* of that' is the mantra that should be made to work.

A car customer goes to a particular showroom's website to decide on the purchase of a vehicle. He then visits a few showrooms and skips the one he visited on the internet. The people at the showroom missed the reason and have to work out why that customer didn't come to that showroom. They have to figure out what is it that the other showrooms are offering which they aren't. Once that is done, the website can be revamped to suit the needs of the customer and create a new circumstance for a change in behaviour. It is possible the website was attracting the wrong people—those who were not serious customers but casual visitors to the site. To make the casual serious, the showroom can redesign the website to make it more appealing.

If a smoker finds that purchasing a pack of cigarettes has become difficult because the cigarette shops are away from his place of work or home, he will delay his urge. Or, even if he visits a shop further away, he would do it less often. All of this is possible if the intermediate steps are broken down and understood.

What do these intermediate steps involve? First, the decision to buy the pack. Second, find a place to smoke, away from office or home. Third, open the pack. Fourth, remove a cigarette. Fifth, light it. If there is a break in any of these intermediate steps, the final act of smoking can be disrupted. Interventions that had not occurred before, present themselves as possible solutions.

When Maruti Suzuki came out with its 800cc small car, the Indian automobile market was dominated by the ubiquitous Ambassador and Premier Padmini. They were everywhere—in government offices, in private households and as cabs. But the 800cc car was an instant hit because it looked compact and neat. It also promised better technology and, most importantly for the Indian market, fuel efficiency.

Encouraged, Maruti began to roll out bigger cars, the sedans and other hatchbacks. But it ran into competition from Hyundai, which entered the market with its Santro and Accent models. What did Maruti do? It studied on the intermediate steps that a potential buyer goes through before making the final act of purchasing. Maruti Suzuki developed a vast network of sales and service outlets so that the customer had only to look up, and he would see the company's logo nearly everywhere. The number of motor mechanics trained was so enormous that you had mechanics spread along the national highways familiar with the repair of Maruti Suzuki vehicles. The customer was offered a peace of mind while travelling.

Associated ideas were also triggered by some intelligent and aggressive marketing. Maruti became a 'family car', a vehicle that happy families travelled in and saw places. A car that could be taken for a long pleasurable drive as well as for commute to the office. The fact that it was compact and could not contain a large family was not allowed to become a negative.

Over the years, while the sales of Hyundai grew significantly, Maruti retained its top position. It built on associations, it brought attention to related behaviours and it triggered emotions. And importantly, it made good use of the cascading effect—the large number of Maruti buyers propelled the desire in others to own one as well.

5

MEET THE DESIRES

Management guru and author of the best-seller, *How to Win Friends and Influence People*, Dale Carnegie had once said, 'The only way on earth to influence people is to talk about what they want, and show them how to get it.'[11]

His words turned on its head the conventional wisdom of persuading people. He had not conducted any scientific experiment to arrive at the universal truth but had drawn from his own experience and intuition. But research done over the recent years have proved he was dead right. It is difficult to make people do what you want. But if you talk in their language and understand what they want, you can give it to them, and that would be relatively easy.

Take the example of a television salesman. He holds forth at great length the dazzling advantages of an OLED system. As far as he is concerned, the lure is so great that no customer in his right frame of mind would refuse to buy such a wonderful product. Imagine his surprise when the customer appears uninterested. Where did the salesman go wrong?

He was so carried away by what he believed was what the

---

[11]Dale Carnegie, *How to Win Friends and Influence People*, RHUK, 2004.

customer needed that he forgot to understand what *actually* the customer wanted. If he had cared to listen to the customer, he would have known that the poor fellow was merely interested in a high-definition television set that did not burn a hole in his pocket. He was not interested in OLED. Had the salesman grasped that, he could have guided the customer to an array of brands that provide what the customer wanted and closed the sale. Instead, to his dismay, the customer simply walked out of the showroom without making a purchase. He was put off by the salesman's insistence on making him want something that he did not want.

Persuasion does not always mean changing what people want. The salesman wants the closure of a sale. He can do so by listening to what the customer wants and giving it. The salesman should pursue what the customer desires, not what he wants to sell to the customer.

Some car manufacturers promote their cars as speedy, exciting and full of adrenaline-pumping action. This might attract the male customer, but his wife may not be so delighted. She may want safety and enough room for the family to go on outings. She would be interested in comfort more than speed. It would be foolhardy for the company's sales team to try to change the female customer's behaviour in favour of speed and excitement. Instead, he must speak to the woman about the advanced safety features and great legroom that the car has. Thus, it has features that can keep both the husband and the wife satisfied.

The parents want their children to be disciplined and away from negative influences that too much freedom can bring. On the other hand, the young want more freedom and less control of their parents, because they believe they are old enough to take decisions regarding themselves. Both are right in their own respective ways, and yet, there is a clash. The student wants to drop out of college, because he believes his calling is elsewhere. The parent cannot convince him to do otherwise by saying that his calling is wrong. If the parent does that, it will only further add to the child's determination to drop out. Instead, the father (or mother) could try explaining to the child that his calling can be better realized once he graduates from college. Accept the child's ambition and show him the right way to fructify it.

In both the above cases, the persuader has to appreciate what the other person wants and fulfil that desire—instead of trying to make the person do what you want.

In a college hostel dormitory, students used the air-conditioner liberally, even when it was not needed; it was more out of habit than need. The college Dean made several attempts to persuade the inmates that the overuse of air-conditioners was bad for the environment—he gave them high-sounding statistics to make his point. The pep talk did not work and the students continued with their habit. Neither their attitude nor their act changed.

The Dean then applied another technique. At the end of a month, he sat down with the students in a seminar and showed them the electricity bills. He explained that the bill amount could be reduced by half every month if they used the air-conditioners sparingly. The savings could be utilized to improve the facilities in the hostel, such as better beds, work tables and a new badminton court—as well as a swimming pool in the premises. The trick worked, of course.

In large parts of rural regions across the world, especially in developing and less-developed countries, the use of low power consumption electric appliances such as light bulbs are popular, because the predominant factor is low electricity bill. CFLs are, thus, much in demand; the fact that it is also environment-friendly is not the overriding circumstance for the reason for buying.

Sometimes, messages have quite the opposite effect than desired. For example, certain categories of people are put off by constant reminders about environment-friendliness. If a product comes with a label of being environment-friendly, they look at it with suspicion—perhaps it is less efficient. They could be conservatives who believe that the pro-environment lobby is overstating the environment issue agenda and is busy with pushing its own agenda for secretive purposes.

On the other hand, if a product does not have a favourable environment-related star rating, the liberals or the environmentalists will frown upon such products, even if those products have environment-friendly technology.

Remove the label and the product becomes more acceptable, even if expensive. Put the label and the product becomes less acceptable. Give people what they want and they will accept it. It is about fulfilling desires and not changing them.

What happens when a persuader is faced with two groups of people who have different desires? There is no point in trying to work out a compromise. Talk to the groups separately. If you have no option but to address them commonly, try checking out common desires—there must be at least some—and persuading them. Giving them different rewards will not work.

While on environment, take the instance of recycling. The liberals will see environmental-friendliness in them while the conservatives will see cost-saving. It is tempting to offer both the incentives to a common group of liberals and conservatives, but neither will work in tandem. It is because different people see different rewards separately and not as an 'average'—which is appealing. However, the matter does not simplify itself by a separation of groups alone. People may want more than one reward, and the persuader has to choose that which is most appealing and persuasive.

Promise the Big Reward

When persuading a person to do an act, we are worried that offering a huge incentive could make the person sceptical and thus unwilling to change his behaviour. That is a mistake. Small rewards are actually disincentivizing. Then, you will have to offer another reward, another promise, but that may not have appeal.

Award-winning novelist Kristin Hannah said, 'Promises were a lot like impressions. The second one didn't count for much.'[12] The first promise of a reward holds the maximum potency, and the persuader must ensure that he promises the best and the biggest reward right up front.

Imagine telling a middle-class family that it would save $10 a month if it were to cut down on the use of television or air conditioning. It won't cut ice; on the contrary, the reward would be greeted with contempt. By telling the family members that they could save enough in a year to fund a short vacation, they would be receptive.

If you tell an overweight school child that he will become healthy by giving up on potato chips, it will not work. But he could be convinced if you point out to him that, by giving up on potato chips, he can be fit enough so that fellow students stop making fun of him. The child is more sensitive to criticism

---

[12]Kristin Hannah, *Distant Shores*, Ballantine Books, 2003.

from his friends in school than about being unhealthy. The big reward for him is an end to the humiliation in school.

The elderly has a problem with smart phones because they are seen as complicated. In order to appeal to their desires, you have to persuade them to see the user-friendly features in the phones and make them comfortable. That is their big reward. If you lecture them on the power that the smart phone holds in influencing people across the globe through the use of social media, they will not be as impressed—for that prospect is a small reward for them. On the other hand, what is a small reward for the elderly is a big reward for the young. They will not be persuaded by ease of use; the young can unravel the functioning of technology in a phone within minutes of using it.

The best rewards are those that are universally acceptable; that which most people want is bound to click for all segments of society. Parents want to present themselves as role models for their children. Teachers want their students to be good at studies. Scientists and researchers want recognition and breakthroughs in their work to be known across a wide spectrum of people. Such strong motives are universal, and while there could be differences in their desires, they would be trivial in comparison and not worth considering. The risk in taking them into account is to veer away from the larger promise of a reward.

Marketing professionals often work at segmenting their target groups according to their preferences, age, education, etc. That may be useful, but they also run the risk of magnifying even the minor differences that exist among the groups. Once they do the grouping, the marketers tend to miss the big picture and miss the wood for the trees. The consequence is that they fail to evolve strategies that offer the big rewards to the people in all segments.

Melinda Gates said, 'I want them to see that in the universal human desire to be happy, to develop our gifts, to contribute to others, to love and be loved—we're all the same. Nobody is any better than anybody else, and no one's happiness or human dignity matters more than anyone else's.'

What Are Universal Desires?

Leading psychologist Abraham Maslow did pioneer research on universal desires eight decades ago. He concluded that as humans, we share certain common basic needs that relate to physiology, safety, emotions of love, belonging and self-esteem, and the realization of our needs.

Research has told us that individuals prioritize the universal desires according to their needs and perceptions. Steven Ross, a psychologist, propounded his theory of universal desires and motivations, said that

> Individuals differ enormously in what makes them happy—for some competition, winning and wealth are the greatest sources of happiness, but for others, feeling competent or socialising may be more satisfying. The point is that you can't say some motivations are inherently inferior.[13]

He added that labelling certain motivations as 'good' and others 'bad' is akin to imposing one's value system on others. But of course, any behaviour or desire that is harmful to the self or others are undesirable.

---

[13] Jeff Grabmeier, 'Intrinsic Motivation Doesn't Exist, Researcher Says', OSU. EDU, 8 May 2005, https://news.osu.edu/intrinsic-motivation-doesnt-exist-researcher-says/, Accessed on 1 April 2022.

The persuaders must strive to understand what the other person's 'true desire' is, rather than question them on 'why' that is so. Because, asking 'what' rather than 'why' is one important step towards better awareness of the other person's needs and acts.

The research to understand universal human desires began in the early twentieth century with William McDougall, a social psychologist at Harvard University. Many lists and ideas since then have evolved on the subject, with experts seeking to understand how they drive an individual or a group's goal-oriented behaviour.

Psychologist Stephen Reiss identified 16 universal human desires. At the same time, he added that individuals have their own goals, priorities and values.

Maslow maintained the first level of requirement or desire was physiological—the need of water, food, warmth, sleep, etc. The next level of need arises once those are taken care of. Among them is safety. Economic security, safety of life and property. The need for belonging comes next. Family, friends, lovers and a general acceptance in society. That involves recognition, prestige, awards, etc. The final need, so to say, is that of self-actualization involving fresh challenges, creativity, innovation, etc. If one were to draw a pyramid of needs, the base would be physiological and the tip on the top would comprise of self-actualization.

Desires can be self or intrinsic, in which the subject wants something for its own sake; or instrumental, where the subject seeks for the sake of something else. 'Standing desires' are always at the back of the mind—in a non-conscious way—whereas 'occurrent desires' arise consciously. There are higher desires which relate to spiritual or religious goals while the lower desires have to do with material pleasures. The jury is still out on whether desires are the practical reasons or if there can be practical reasons without a desire to follow them. I may have a practical reason to buy a car, but do I really have a desire to own the car?

Marketing and advertising companies have made use of psychological research on the stimulation of desire. Desire is at the heart of novels and films, especially where social or cultural norms are challenged, and desires of love and romance of friendship are sabotaged or sought to be sabotaged.

Universal behaviour is one that is common to all humans—of different societies, cultural and social backgrounds. If we understand those behaviours, we can infer the universal desires. In his book, *Human Universals*, anthropologist Donald Brown provides a rather long list of desires and behaviours that ranges from a desire to enhance status, the need to reciprocate the desire to be attractive, to possess what others have, be seen as superior from others to even misleading people at times.[14]

There are complications, no doubt, but if we read Maslow and Brown together, we see that the principle remains the same—whether we target an individual or a group of people. Take two scenarios. The first lists the desires of people that the persuader wants to persuade into a certain type of action. The second scenario represents the positives that can happen if the target (individual or group) acts the way you want him/them to act. Health can be a desire, and the positive outcome can be if the target acts on healthy habits such as purchasing and consuming health food or using quality jogging shoes. If the desire is to feel superior, the target can act to buy an expensive car that his neighbours do not own.

There can also be an overlap of desires and outcomes, and the

---

[14] Donald Brown, *Human Universals*, McGraw-Hill Education, 1991.

rewards that you plan will have to take into consideration those overlaps. You have to persuade people that your recommendation for an action is the optimum one to realize their desires.

Your son does not want to stay in a boarding school, but you believe that a boarding school is the best option for him to do well in studies and also develop a sense of discipline. The reward you have to offer to convince him has to have an outcome of agreeing to boarding school and also to meet his desire. He may desire to play video games, but that is not an outcome of choosing to stay in a boarding school. The outcome could be to enhance discipline in your child, but that may not be his desire. Since these do not overlap, you have to find an outcome and desire that overlap.

Freedom from parents' restriction at home can be both an outcome and a desire. The stay in a boarding school frees the child from the constant supervision of his parents—something that he will have desired. And it is also an outcome of staying in a boarding school. Thus, you can have a dialogue with your son on this very tantalizing benefit and convince him to opt for the boarding school. That way, you persuade him to act in the manner you want.

The theory can be applied in other areas as well. Your neighbour has acquired a dog to keep his house safe from thefts and burglary. The dog, in turn, acquires the habit of barking throughout the night. The problem, as far as you are concerned, is that the dog's constant barking disturbs your sleep. The neighbour's dog has become a nuisance, but if you try telling the neighbour that, he is likely to tick you off. He may even argue that the barking keeps your house safe as well. In any case, he doesn't care much if your sleep is disturbed. He is happy enough to hear his dog bark all the time, because he believes that the dog is doing the job it was acquired for.

You could reason with him in a way that does not disturb the reward he seeks—safety. You can tell him that barking through the night does not give any indication to the owner that a thief is nearby. It's more like the story in which a boy cries wolf all the time. It would be safer, you can point out, if the dog barks when a thief is actually lurking around. Timely action can then be taken. For that, the neighbour has to get the dog trained accordingly. This way, both the outcome and reward work in tandem, and the neighbour would get the point.

We Are There

What do most people who buy digital products want? Performance and peace of mind. Computer chip manufacturing company, Intel has effectively understood the consumers' desire. Over decades, it built a reputation for itself and has many computer products with the label, 'Intel Inside' prominently displayed. Just those two words assure the customer of freedom from worry. Many digital products, understanding that Intel had won over public confidence, needed no persuasion to use the chip and proudly proclaim 'Intel Inside' on their products.

But peace of mind or freedom from worry alone, however compelling, could not have swayed customers of digital products. After all, peace of mind is a universal desire, and yet, Intel is less dominating in some countries and more in others. Why the difference? Competitors of Intel could be offering rewards to customers who buy their products—extended warranties, the chance to win a trip to the Maldives, etc.

The digital generation is, nevertheless, different from other customers, and the difference is consistent across continents.

Studies have revealed that the digital generation, primarily comprising the younger lot, love the feel of speed, action and multi-tasking. They are less content with what they have and constantly hanker for upgrades—to their mobile phones, computers and other digital devices. They do not like being anchored to one city, town or one job, always looking to shift and better their stature. In short, the digital generation is restive.

Persuaders, who have understood the overlap of desires and outcome of the digital generation, have done well for themselves. The outcome, for example, of a product could be faster processing. The desire of the customer would be to feel good while using the product. It would be futile for the persuader to harp on the superior technology of a product if the customer is not comfortable in handling the product.

Thus, the possible outcomes have to be in tandem with the desires. The outcome could be emotional, functional or even sensory; and they can be before an action is performed or during the action or after. Let us not forget that the technique of persuasion involves the availability of the action we want the other person to take and the reward that we offer. Reward and outcome must have an association too, as we have seen earlier.

Let's take an example. A country's national dairy development board wants to encourage the habit of consuming more milk products, like butter. The rewards must be positive, of course. But equally important is that the desires and outcomes of the targeted consumer should also match. The following could be some outcomes that may match the desires.

Before consumption, the functional outcome is that butter is a relatively low-cost nutritional option. The emotional outcome could be a special bargain price that is being offered for the festive season. During the action, the functional outcome could be that it is easy to use, not involving cooking. The sensory outcome is that it spreads easily on a slice of bread. The emotional outcome is that it can be used creatively in the kitchen—in a number of dishes. Once the action of consumption is done, the functional outcome is that it provides calcium to the body and strengthens the bones. The sensory outcome would be that consumer would 'feel' healthy, while the emotional outcome is the belief that their family's health is being taken care of.

Those who love soft drinks are driven by many common desires. The physical reward is the drink tastes good, quenches thirst, and makes one feel energized and upbeat. The emotional reward could be that one might get a feeling of being rugged, stylish, tough, intelligent and like a leader.

Most soft drink advertisements promote one or more of these emotional factors. And yet, while soft drink consumers have common desires, they have different choices of brands. That's because they are not in agreement that the other brand fulfils their desires and offers the rewards they are looking for.

Social perceptions—such as ruggedness, manliness, etc.—that get associated with a particular brand are a more determining factor for purchase than the physical attributes of the product, like taste and a sense of refreshment. Various studies have confirmed that social perceptions have almost twice as much potency as the physical. A soft drink manufacturer's promotional campaign that focuses largely on matters of taste, a feeling of refreshment, etc. will not work as well as a campaign that emphasizes on social rewards.

Of course, if the target audience is feeling physically drained—is thirsty, tired, hungry, drowsy—then the physical characteristics can kick into play. But even here, the social rewards can work in the background.

It has been found in researches that both the young and elderly are motivated by social perceptions. However, the younger lot is more influenced by them, whereas the older men are less turned by perceptions of manliness or ruggedness.

The importance of social perceptions is relevant to other products as well, such as cell phones, computers or automobiles. The pattern that was evident in the case of soft drinks exists for other products too.

Rewards are enticing for sure. But there are at least two other factors that are important in connection with the rewards. One, what is the surety of the reward? And two, how soon would the rewards come? The automatic system wants quick results, because its choices are also made in a spur-of-the-moment.

Immediate Rewards

If I were to give you a choice between accepting $500 or $200, what would you do? It's a no-brainer really—you would opt for five hundred dollars. However, if I were to ask you to choose between $200 that you can get now, or $500 that you will get after six months, the response would be different, isn't it? You would settle for two hundred now. That's the power of immediacy. Outcomes that can happen here and now are more attractive than the distant outcomes.

The persuader who understands the power of immediate outcomes succeeds better than the one who promises future rewards. If a salesman wants a low-income customer to purchase CFL bulbs instead of the incandescent ones, there is no point is telling him that he will save enough money in a year that can fetch him two gas cylinders. Instead, emphasize on how much he can save in a month—enough that can buy his daughter a new school uniform.

It is a fact that many times, distant rewards are better in long-term, whereas the immediate rewards have only short-term benefits. For instance, saving for retirement is a distant reward, but it can be life-defining in many ways. So is the benefit to quit smoking—the long-term reward is better health, especially in old age when health-related matters have the tendency to constantly prop up.

However, even that can be achieved by talking of immediate gains. If you save today, the immediate reward is that you do not spend on needless goods. If you quit smoking, the instant reward is that you end the constant niggling of your spouse.

Certain Rewards

Certain rewards must not be confused with distant gains. The latter is a certainty, even if in the future. But there is also something that is an uncertain reward, however attractive. Take the following example. There is a certainty that you will get $100 extra on an investment. In another option, there is a 75 per cent certainty that you will get an extra $60 and a 40 per cent certainty that you will gain another $80. The choice for you is the sure $100 and lesser sure is the $140.

Rationality would dictate that the second option is worth taking the risk for because of the expected value. But 90 per cent of the people would opt for the first. Because a certain reward is more motivating than an uncertain one, even if the uncertain reward is higher. The 'one bird in hand is worth two in a bush' mindset comes into play. In fact, even if a delayed reward is certain and higher in value, most people would prefer the immediate one, even if lower in estimation.

If the immediate reward is certain at 'X' and the delayed reward is 'X plus 2' but equally certain, the tilt would be towards the immediate. This is because the certainty of the delayed could be marred by unexpected and unforeseen developments. This is the automatic system at work.

All of these do not mean that no dilemma exists in the minds of those seeking to be persuaded. Actions that are beneficial to us in the long run versus immediate gains come with another factor. Even if the reward is delayed and uncertain, the cost of immediate gain could be high and deleterious. For instance, if you don't quit smoking now because you find the delayed reward non-enticing, the cost in terms of health is also immediate.

And yet, few people are willing to opt for the delayed rewards and avoid the immediate costs. The persuader has a chance to succeed if he can convert or play down delayed and uncertain rewards in favour of immediate rewards with fewer costs. That can be done by playing on the feelings of the people—feeling, as we have seen earlier, play a dominant role in the automatic system.

In Quest of Uniqueness

Marketers, advertisers and other such persuaders often burn the midnight oil to think of a truly 'unique' reward that their competitors have not thought of yet. They believe that the more novel the reward, the greater would be its acceptance. But this is not always the case.

It's not the newness that makes a reward attractive. All that we have to do is to associate, or link, the reward with the recommended course of action. Link it in such an effective manner that an alternative action is not desired by the target.

Take the case of the soap brands Liril and Lifebuoy, launched by Hindustan Unilever in the Indian market. Liril advertised its product with the all-pervasive 'freshness' as a reward for using it. And Lifebuoy made health the reward. If you wanted to feel freshness soon after a bath, use Liril soaps with varied odours such as that of lemon. If you wished for a feeling of healthiness, it was Lifebuoy. Both freshness and health are timeless rewards, and their relevance remains to this day. Both the brands continue to offer those rewards as associated with the recommended course of action, because they have clicked with audiences over two or three generations. There was nothing unique about these rewards. Most of the later brands of soaps in the Indian market did not attempt to offer anything different; all that they did was to introduce a new tagline, but essentially, the focus was on health and freshness.

Let's take the case of household batteries in the US market. The competition for many years has been between Duracell and Energizer. Duracell latched on to the 'long-lasting' reward early on in its campaign. Energizer took a different tack. It claimed that listening to your music devices becomes more rewarding with Energizer batteries. It didn't work, partly because it wasn't really true—the consumer found no difference in their listening experience. Customers buying batteries looked for long-lasting benefits, and so, Energizer abandoned its campaign.

Energizer batteries were as long-lasting as Duracell, but since the latter had opted for and 'owned' the reward earlier on, Energizer could not benefit from that reward. Something had to be done to express that same reward in a different way. An advertising agency finally came up with the Energizer Bunny, which kept beating its drums and cymbals long after the competitors had run out of battery energy. That worked.

Of course, if the reward that the persuader offers is both unique and motivating, there is nothing like it. However, if a choice has to be made, it has to be the motivating one. After all, as we have seen over and over again that persuasion is all about meeting desires, not changing desires. We have to talk about what the target wants and not what you want to thrust down its throat. When we stop showing people what we *think* they want and actually fully invest in what they *really* want, success is assured.

That way, our campaign at persuasion becomes less aggressive, less moralistic and less self-righteous. The target will listen to you when you talk its language—the language of the automatic system.

6

DON'T QUESTION; FIND OUT

To find out what people want, it is necessary to understand what drives the human mind. Josh Kaufman is the author of the best-selling book, *The Personal MBA: Master the Art of Business*. He writes that the best-known general theory of what people want is that which had been propounded by psychologist Abraham Maslow in 1943.

The progress that people make in their needs has been mentioned elsewhere in the book. Each has to be first met in its sequence before the other can be. He had mentioned physiology, safety, belongingness and self-actualization, in that order. But Kaufman prefers what another psychologist Clayton Alderfer's hierarchy of needs or what is referred to as the ERG theory. It is Existence, Relatedness and Growth.

'When people have what they need to survive, they move on to making friends and finding mates. When they are satisfied with their relationships, they focus on doing things they enjoy and improving their skills in things that interest them,' Kaufman says.

He adds that while the ERG theory explains the priority, it does not talk of the methods that need to be used to realize those priorities. 'For that, we must turn to other theories of human action.'[15]

Kaufman quotes Harvard Business School professors Paul Lawrence and Nitin Nohria, who said that all human beings have core human drives, namely, the Drive to Acquire, the Drive to Bond, the Drive to Defend and the Drive to Learn. Kaufman adds another drive: the Drive to Feel. According to him, the desire for 'new sensory stimulus, intense emotional experiences, pleasure, excitement, entertainment and anticipation', is a crucial element in understanding human desires and expectations.

If your product or service offers any of these, or better as many of these as possible, it has good chance of success. In short, an insight into human nature is at the core of personal and business successes.

Role of Insight

But what do we mean by the term 'insight'? Loosely meant, it is anything that offers a fresh perspective on a subject, or an understanding of a process. An insight is generally always revealing. In the study of psychology, we are told that an insight occurs when a solution to a problem comes all of a sudden. This can happen in the wake of several conscious—but failed—attempts to arrive at a solution. A breakthrough with the help of insight often turns out to be more accurate than those which happen without insights.

That said, insight is not a non-scientific phenomenon. Through various studies conducted since the early part of the twentieth century by Gestalt psychology, mechanisms to arrive at insights include seeing a problem from a fresh perspective,

---

[15] Josh Kaufman, *The Personal MBA: Master the Art of Business,* Portfolio, 2012.

associating a problem with another similar problem that has got a solution, exorcizing past experiences that hinder the arrival to a solution or placing the problem in a bigger context and seeking a way out.

Methodical methods exist to study the subject of insight, and they have been used in experiments involving participants who are given problems and puzzles to solve. There are primarily three kinds of methods.

The first is by breaking the functional fixedness, like the 'Duncker's Candle Problem'. Individuals are given matches and a box of tacks. They are told to find a way to attach a candle to the wall to light the room. The box of tacks has to be emptied, the candle set inside the box, the box tacked to the wall, and the candle lighted with the matches. The second method is spatial ability. The famous 'Nine-Dot Problem' offered a good instance. Participants have to draw four lines through nine dots without using a pencil or pen. The third involves the use of verbal ability, like the 'Remote Associates Test'. Individuals have to think of a word that connects three—apparently unrelated—words.

The use of insight into human nature is especially relevant, because quite often, an individual's language hides his real motivation. If a persuader depends on the outer language or attitude of a consumer without understanding what really motivates him into making a decision, he will face failure. The persuader has to know what the target *actually* wants—why he does what he does. Only then can the persuader think of a way to make him change.

It is not always that the consumer does not want to tell what motivates him. At times, he is simply unable to coherently state it. His language camouflages his motivation. He has to be led through the process. He does not know how perceptions and motives, that are not visible, influence our conduct. The automatic system, which influences his behaviour, does not have access to the 'why'. The issue gets more complicated because a person often thinks he knows the 'why', even when he does not. He explains why he behaves the way he does, and he says so with authority and certainty. He believes them to be true.

Of course, this is more so the case with people who have brain-damage issues—people with epilepsy, for instance. Epileptic seizures spread from one hemisphere of the brain to the other, and there is a lack of communication or miscommunication between the two spheres. In a normal brain, there is constant communication between the two hemispheres.

Doctors conducted an interesting experiment on an epileptic patient. They did a surgery by which they disconnected the hemisphere of the brain that had suffered damage from the other. It led to a dramatic improvement in the patient.

People under the spell of hypnosis do things but have no idea why they did it. And yet, they were quick to offer an explanation for their conduct, an explanation that they believed was credible and rational.

David Eagleman is an American neuroscientist, science communicator and author. He is the co-founder of Neurosensory, a firm that develops devices for sensory substitution. According to him, human nature automatically and constantly fabricates stories and narrates them in ways as if the actions related were always our own idea.

An experiment was conducted involving a bunch of participants. A board was put up, which said: 'Choose the best quality.' On the table were five pairs of socks marked A, B, C, D, E. The participants made their choice. When they were asked for the rationale behind their choice, they offered attributes to quality they had found in the socks they chose. Different people had made different choices, and yet every single one of them gave what they believed was clinching evidence of quality. None seemed impressed by the manner in which the socks had been displayed or their colour. The fact was that all five pairs of socks were of the same quality and belonged to the same brand. The only difference was in their colour and positioning on the table.

Now comes the interesting part. The pair of socks placed on the right end of the table were preferred by the maximum number of respondents—more than 40 per cent. The positioning had clearly worked as a determinant, but no participant admitted to their choice based on the position. Instead, they rationalized their decision by quoting qualities that were fabricated in their minds but which they genuinely believed to be true.

This brings us to the crux of the chapter: 'Reported versus Revealed'. What is Reported is what the target tells us. It could be fabricated, supposedly rational, and considered as the truth by the target. But the Revealed is what lies behind the language or the conduct. It is often a surprising find, and thus, an Insight.

Why do you find a certain person attractive and another, not so? The answer would be easy to give; that you find someone attractive or not attractive, is easier to state.

A young female interviewer approaches a bunch of men and hands them a questionnaire. The questions are simple enough: what food they prefer to eat, what clothes they like to wear, whether they like to party and do they like reading books? This, she does while seated in a park bench.

Then, she approaches another set of men and does the same; this time standing and allowing the gentle breeze to caress her flowing hair and skirt.

The female interviewer then leaves her phone number with each of the participants and asks them to call her in case they need to know more about the exercise.

The maximum number of callers came from the group that she had approached while standing in the breeze. The Reported reason was that they were interested in knowing more about the social exercise they had been part of. But the Revealed reason was that they had been attracted by her physical persona when she allured them while standing as the breeze caressed her hair and dress. They could not admit that they were bowled over by her dress or the way she posed, her smile or her way of talking. They could not say that their heart was beating rapidly as she spoke with them.

The conscious mind does not know why we do what we do, because the conscious is not involved in the way we behave in a certain manner. Therefore, we are unable to express the real motives and fall back on the Reported reasons.

If people don't know why they do what they do, should not the persuader try to pry that secret by directly asking them? He can do it, but it will lead him nowhere. Worse, it could lead him in the wrong direction. The information he gets would be flawed and would, in turn, lead to erroneous conclusions. All of that would add to the persuader failing in his task.

Our automatic, non-conscious mind considers even the wrong reasons as true and expresses them with conviction, thus misleading the persuader. Even professionals such as media personnel often find it hard to resist the temptation of considering as true a great amount of information that they gather. The more experienced ones, of course, dig deeper and discreetly to get to the Revealed reason.

Now we know that 'why' is the wrong tactic to use, and

yet, most persuaders use it frequently. Look at the research exercises conducted by professional agencies, and you will find 'why' prominently in the questionnaire. The field staff has to provide answers to their superiors, and if the 'why' can get them those answers, they will use it. The problem is, such answers are incorrect, and the agency ends up coming to wrong conclusions about the target audience they have in mind. This is also one of the reasons why pollsters often get their opinion polls wrong. They are asking the wrong questions, motivated by the 'why'.

A good example of that is the opinion polls conducted in the US when Donald Trump was running for President. Most of them predicted a defeat for Trump because the 'why' elected the response that the voters were looking for experience and a proven track record—which Republican candidate Trump did not have. And yet, as polls neared, everybody realized that Trump was not only the frontrunner but that his ratings were higher than his opponents—including the Democrat Hillary Clinton.

The question now arises: if we do not know why people do what they do, what is the way to get to the truth?

Finding the Truth

One tested, tried and successful way is to ask people questions on other issues and get their responses. These would be questions that do not require crafty responses. The responses to those questions can help the persuader to understand why people do what they do and also get the target to change without directly asking the relevant question.

A good way to begin the exercise is to list out the most probable reasons why some people already do what the persuader wants them to do. The people may prefer one political candidate over the other, one brand over the other, one mobile service over the other, etc. They may have stopped consuming alcohol, given up smoking or eating junk food.

Then talk to all those people who have 'changed'. Don't ask them directly why they have changed, but seek out their response on what they think about the options. Ask them of their opinion on what they think of people who do what they (the changed ones) do or what they don't do that you would like them to do. You must not just listen to the answers but observe them closely to understand the desires that motivated them towards change.

An elaborate exercise, such as the one above, will reveal a lot of information. Evaluate that information and come to some conclusions—you will be able to better understand the motives of the people who have changed. You can identify the rewards that worked, the aspirations that clicked. However, if you were to ask them the 'why' directly, you will end up in a blind alley.

You can then identify the rewards that are relevant to the target audience that you wish to engage with, because there are good chances that those same rewards will work in the new situation as well. And if they don't, you can always try out a different reward.

Let's say that you want a man to quit smoking. Your internal analysis of the data from the person you talked with—the one who had quit smoking—reveals that he feels good to have contributed to the health of his beloved family members who were earlier exposed to the fumes of tobacco. That is the reward which motivated him. You can then use that as a reward for the person you want to persuade to stop smoking. If that does not work well, then you have to think of something else.

You can fall back on what we discussed earlier in this book.

Find the target desires and the action outcomes, and look for an overlap. What does your target desire that can be had out of the action you want him to take? Make sure you don't ask him directly—use the indirect method.

If the smoker is concerned more about his own health, emphasize on the benefits of giving up smoking. You can even amplify the dangers such as cancer. Hospitalization, high costs of treatment, the pain and the agony. Associate all of these to smoking.

Using air-conditioners that consume less electricity may be appealing to those who use such products because they have seen the results. But that might not motivate those who don't yet use them. Study closely what they desire, and you can find the right reward that you can project. It is possible that the consumer is not enamoured to lower power bills—he can afford the higher costs—but he could be motivated if you can show him that the energy-efficient air-conditioners are suitable for his locality which suffers from low voltage issues.

The Munch & Crunch Case

Let's consider a hypothetical example, that of the Munch & Crunch fast food joint. Here, your target is not one customer but many. You have quite a few customers but would like more. Since word-of-mouth publicity is a good way to promote the restaurant, you would like your existing customers to recommend the joint to their friends. But how do you make them do that?

Begin with the basics. Prepare a list of the probable reasons why your customer should recommend your restaurant. Read on the subject and list out the best guesses of others. Other similar fast-food joints will have done some research, so you can read them. But make sure that the research findings are not based on the direct 'why', because that will give you the wrong conclusions.

Having done the ground work, which market researchers call 'secondary research', you might arrive at a bunch of reasons why your customer would recommend the restaurant to a friend. It could be the following: food quality, competitive prices, friendly service, competent staff, prompt service and a variety of dishes to choose from.

Armed with this list, conduct a random survey among your customers on each of these attributes, not forgetting to ask how many of them would like to recommend the restaurant to their friends. You can also ask them to rank the reasons according to their priority.

Let's now assume that most of the customers listed the quality of food as the most important criterion, followed by competitive prices. Had you guessed that your customers would recommend based on the quality of food, without giving the customers the choice of attributes, you might not have come to an accurate understanding. Once you know that a customer places quality of food as his top priority, you know that quality is the essence in the customer making the recommendation.

However, there is something more here. What the customers responded was the Reported. The customer believed that his response on quality of food was rational. But it is possible that the Revealed was something else—it could be the prompt service, or the friendly nature of the serving staff. This is not to say that people don't care about quality—they do. But that may not have been good enough reason to recommend the fast-food joint to a friend. There could be other restaurants that serve good quality food but the staff there may not be friendly or the service may not be prompt.

There is a connection between perception and the likelihood of recommendation, but that does not necessarily mean that the perception triggered the recommendation. But an absence of connection at least means that the perception is immaterial and you can eliminate it from your consideration. If the perception is not connected with what people do, it can be safely assumed that that perception is not resulting in a change in behaviour. We can consider, as an instance, the perception of prompt service at the Munch & Crunch outlet. If people who say the service is slow and those who say the service is prompt are equally willing to recommend the fast-food joint, then clearly the perception of fast service is irrelevant.

Also, if nearly everyone says that the service is good, then nearly every one of those should be recommending the restaurant to their friend. If they don't, then that perception is immaterial. Similarly, if almost everyone claims that the service is lax, then none from that group should be giving the outlet a thumbs up. Yet, if some among them recommend the outlet, then again, the perception served no purpose.

There is a third situation that provides a more complicated link between perception and the possibility of recommendation. What if people who think the service is slow also recommend the fast-food joint to their friends, along with those who consider the service fast? And, those who hold the model ground—service is neither particularly slow or fast—are unlikely to recommend?

In either of the three cases, the perception of promptness of service does not matter, because it has little persuasive value. There is an absence of relationship, of a connection. Therefore, that perception got discounted in the persuader's scheme of things.

External factors can also play a role in perceptions. For instance, the perception of the staff being friendly. This would be more emphatic if the customers happened to be friends or relatives of the staff. It is, in effect, not the friendliness *per se* but a new variable that influences perception and behaviour. Such perceptions also need not be taken at face value by the persuader in crafting his strategy.

When we like a restaurant, we can always think of various reasons (perceptions) to justify our decision. But when a couple of perceptions are considered positive in recommending while the others are not, then those perceptions cannot be taken as reliable. And so, if the quality of food is not that good but the perception is that the staff is friendly, the recommendation would still come. If the prices are on the higher side but the perception is that the service is good, the recommendation could still come.

What is the final take of this exercise, then? The best way to increase the number of recommendations is to promote the perception that Munch & Crunch employees are friendly and the service is good. We have thus unearthed the Revealed reason.

The Blaze Card Case

We may consider another hypothetical example. Those were the days when Blaze credit cards were already in use, but the customers used it rarely. This was not because people did not want to use credit cards but because they used cards other than Blaze as their first preference. Blaze was there as a backup. The Blaze management wanted to change that behaviour and make their card the first choice of customers.

The management team began making a list of the most

probable reasons for the likely preference of Blaze among customers who owned the card. Some of the explanations that were offered, by way of association with the card, were as follows:

- Low annual fees
- Low interest rates
- Wide acceptance across various merchant outlets
- Cashback choices on purchases
- Savings plan, with an offer for a savings account on the card
- Image of a classy customer; the card looked dazzling and was associated with the image of a classy user

The survey then sought to get responses from Blaze card customers on their perceptions about the card and their preference. The idea was to find which of the perceptions led to Blaze being the first choice.

The surveyors discovered that the proportion of customers who made Blaze their preference was nearly the same among those who believed the card had a low annual fee as it was among people who did not share that perception. Similarly, the preference was the same among those who thought the interest rate was low and the customers who did not. Interestingly, the preference was low among people who 'thought' Blaze had a wider acceptance. In other words, customers who preferred Blaze used it more often and faced rejections.

Again, those who made Blaze their first choice because of the associated image of the card were in the same proportion as those who did not subscribe to the classy image. The same was the case with the savings plan offer. It turned out from the survey that the only perception that was positively associated with the preference given to Blaze was the cashback offer. Thus, those who were likely to make Blaze their first choice was driven most by the perception of cashback offers. This was the association that was the motivator.

The management quickly junked its earlier campaign that listed out a host of rewards and confused the customer. That campaign had failed to capitalize on the one most captivating association. The new promotional drive concentrated exclusively on the cashback offer, listing reasons why it was better than what was being given by its competitors. The strategy worked, and Blaze sales grew five-fold over the next seven years.

Say Cheese

The Dairy Products Board, set up by the Parliament of India, was looking for an advertising agency to promote its brand of cheese. A relatively new and mid-sized ad firm was also in the race, and it was called to make its pitch. There was two months to go for the D-day and the agency had to be ready with its sample advertisement campaign. Its young but enthusiastic creative team took the sensible first step: market research—not by directly asking 'why' but by unearthing that 'why'.

It issued with some accuracy that women of the house had a major say in the dishes being served at home. Getting people who reject cheese would be a tough nut to crack; getting them to serve the product would be a non-starter. Women who, even if occasionally, served cheese could be made to serve it more often. The agency had a number of working hypotheses, some of which are listed below:

- **Nutritional Benefits.** Women who served cheese only at times had a low perception of the health benefits of the

product (calcium, protein, etc.) than women who served it frequently.
- **Nutritional Drawbacks.** Women who served cheese less often perceived that it had health concerns (such as calories and fat) than those who served cheese dishes more often.
- **Taste.** Women who served cheese occasionally did not have a positive outlook on its taste than those who served it often.
- **Cost.** Cheese was seen as an expensive option by women who served it less often than those who served its regularly.
- **Recipe Options.** The awareness of the many recipes that cheese could command was less among women who served the product less often than among women who served it more often.

Remember, these were the perceptions that we believed could be the reasons for the low intake of cheese among households.

The field staff of the advertising agency began to interview women after ascertaining that they served cheese to their families. They were asked as to how often they served cheese and their related perceptions and understanding of the product.

It was found that women who served occasionally and those who served it regularly had the same perception of the product's nutritional benefits and nutritional drawbacks. They were happy with the health benefits and not too concerned about the health negatives. Similarly, both groups of women liked the taste and believed it was worth the price. Thus, neither price nor nutritional value nor taste as perceptions determined the frequency of use, either way.

The field personnel discovered that their hypothesis of recipe options made the difference. Women who served it only occasionally were not aware of the many easy ways by which cheese could be used in the preparation of many dishes, but women who used it often were aware. This discovery led to another corollary—women who used cheese less often were less experienced cooks and less confident of trying out new cheese dishes. Therefore, this was the perception that made the difference.

The agency made its sales pitch: the advertising must focus on giving women easy to make cheese-serving solutions. The Dairy Products Board agreed and a new campaign was crafted accordingly. One of the campaigns claimed that peas could be turned into 'super peas' with cheese; another said that a bit of melted cheese could make the broccoli 'just disappear'. The tagline was: 'Don't forget the cheese!' This was specifically directed at occasional cheese servers. The campaign worked and the sales of the Board's cheese products grew rapidly in a matter of months.

Had the agency directly asked the 'why' of serving cheese often or less often, it would have gotten many, perfectly rational answers, but none would have been the Revealed one. They would have made complete sense to the respondent but would have been far from the actual truth—and with little connection with the behaviour of the respondents. With a wrong conclusion, efforts at behavioural change would not have worked, and the agency would have been on the wrong track.

We had, earlier in the book, spoken about the need to change the act rather than the attitude. The 'say cheese' example exemplifies the power of that approach. Here, attitude was not the impediment, because the target had a positive attitude towards cheese (nutrition, taste, price, etc.) The impediment was non-access to easy-to-serve methods. Once that was resolved, the behaviour changed.

It is important here to reassert that people don't intentionally mislead us with Reported reasons. They are simply certain that the reasons they provide to the direct 'why' are rational and genuine.

French mathematician and philosopher Blaise Pascal said, 'The heart has its reasons which reason knows not'.

The clever persuader never directly asks. He digs and discovers.

7
EMOTION IS THE KEY

It is generally believed that emotions and rational thinking cannot go hand-in-hand; and that clear thinking is the outcome of a lack of emotional feelings. Philosophers such as Plato and several centuries later, David Hume, held the view that emotion and rationality were conflicting opposites. For instance, one can act irrationally in anger or in despair.

However, later research has shown that emotions can channelize into rational thoughts and actions too. Anger could have been a useful stimulus of aggression in the prehistoric era, but it can lead to constructive actions in modern times too.

As a general rule, emotions do play a significant role in people's personal and social lives. Even Hume admitted that reason by itself does not act as a motivator to moral behaviour. Emotions do.

Modern research in neuroscience has also arrived at a similar conclusion. Noted neurologist, Antonio Damasio, who has done pioneering work in understanding the connection between emotions or feelings and action, believes that emotions have a major role to play in taking correct decisions.

Contrary to belief, people who do not have the ability to feel emotions are more likely to make poorer choices. Damasio said that people with emotions do not lose the ability to make rational choices; that faculty remains intact. What gets added is the emotional quotient.

In fact, many experiments conducted by him have concluded that people who makes choices through the automatic system arrive at advantageous situations without knowing beforehand what the advantageous strategy is.

One experiment involved participants gambling with four decks of cards. Two of the decks were riskier than the others. Thus, opening the cards of two decks led to more frequent rewards while the other two resulted in losses. The participants did not know the difference, but after a while, they began choosing the decks that were more gainful. While contemplating the risky decks, they would get fidgety and uneasy, thus expressing an emotion that led to their making the correct choices and avoiding the risky ones. The non-conscious automatic system had kicked into action, leading the participants to an advantageous position and keeping away from the risky ones.

We have come across earlier in the book about experiments with brain-damaged patients. They felt no emotion and thus could not avoid the wrong choices.

Often, we get answers to the questions of what people want through attributes: less calories, more taste, happy family, etc. These are relevant, but if we scale up our research, we can take this a level higher. We can understand the way that the attributes make us feel. The automatic system responds more to how a particular attribute makes us feel rather than the attribute itself.

Show Them Their Way to Feel

We have seen how a persuader can show people how to get what they want by seeking answers in the indirect way. The 'showing people how to get what they want' can be rearranged to also mean 'showing people how to feel the way they would like to feel'. This is important because, and we have seen, emotions play a big role in actions and behaviour, and can lead to a change in attitude as well.

The attributes are important, but even more so is the next, higher step—feelings. Why do customers prefer 'Intel Inside'? Because it improves the speed of processing. When that happens, work gets done faster. And when work gets done after, one can move on to the next task more swiftly. Taken together, the entire process results in a positive feeling.

Let's consider the hypothetical example of Presto, a soft drink brand which has a regional presence. It's less expensive than multinational brands such as Coca Cola or Pepsi. It comes in a number of flavours, unlike the better known two brands.

The variety in flavour was a big add-on. But this attribute had to be scaled up to the level of feeling. The advertising agency, tasked with promoting the brand, understood the matter immediately. It realized that Presto could be projected in a more appealing manner because consumers prefer variety—a number of choices. The variety empowers the consumer and gives him a feeling of being in command in terms of choice.

The ad agency created a number of campaigns that revolved around the variety of flavours, including attractive jingles. Soon, the campaign also included the attribute of low prices and created a package of choice and low price that neither Coke nor Pepsi could boast about. The campaign worked and sales of Presto went up considerably.

Although the success was short-lived, Presto could not match the muscle power and penetration level of the multinational brands in the long run. The experiment showed that scaling up feeling does work. The 'same old taste' versus the 'choice of flavours' was taking attributes to the level of emotions or feeling.

Why do persuaders have to work so hard at scaling up attributes to the level of feeling? Can the target not do it? After all, it is the consumer who experiences the attributes.

The target cannot be expected to do so, because the target sees the attribute. The feelings have to be aroused by a third party. Let's say Company A is engaged in water-proofing solutions and is the market leader. Good water-proofing means less hassles of seepages, inside and on the outer walls of the building. It means that residents can plan their interiors without fear of water seepages ruining their efforts.

These are all attributes, but they have to be translated into feelings. The feeling is that of the peace of mind of planning interior work, even if the resident has no plan of doing the interiors of his house.

An elaborate security system in a residential colony means less chances of burglary. It means the filtering of people who visits the residential flats in the colony. It means constant coverage by CCTV cameras. These are all attributes. The feeling for a resident is that, when he leaves home for an out-of-station trip, he immediately feels that his home is secure. This feeling comes even if the resident has no plans to travel outside.

People install chimneys in their kitchens. The attribute is that the chimney sucks out the smoke that comes when cooking is done and keeps the kitchen smoke-free and fresh. The feeling is one of satisfaction, even when there is no cooking done.

A focus on feelings means that you can get a person to believe that he has more control. A food product that has a low-calorie content gives the feeling of healthiness. A smoke-detector gives the feeling of security. A soft drink brand with multiple flavours gives the feeling of control over choice. Parents often tell their children that a good college education can fetch them attractive jobs or higher salaries. The two are attributes that can work as a reward also. But it is possible that children, being children, may be rebellious to the idea of what they may see as a monotonous life derived from the cushion of job security and good money. They may want to be adventurous, do something non-traditional, and want recognition and pride.

Scaling up the attributes of high salary and good jobs to the level of feelings can be done to persuade children. They can be told that good money and secure jobs could give them the freedom to indulge in their favourite activities and gain recognition and respect. If we know that the child desires freedom, respect and recognition, then we have to translate the attributes into feelings.

By focusing on feeling, we not only convert an attribute (which can also be a rational reward) into an emotional reward, but we also make a delayed and uncertain reward sound like one that is immediate and certain. As we have earlier, a delayed reward, even if certain and good in the long-run, is likely to be passed over for an immediate and sometimes, not a lasting good reward.

Economic models tell us that the attraction of benefits from rewards declines with time, and often, that decline happens rapidly. Take the case of hunger. The reward is food, and once food is had, the attraction for food as a reward disappears. Sleep is another reward that appeals to a person who has not slept for long. But once his sleep is taken care of, the appeal of sleep as a reward dissipates. These are what psychologists call as 'visceral rewards'. Here, the immediate is more pronounced that afterwards, the later has no meaning or appeal. There is no point in telling a sleep-deprived person that he can get sleep after 48 hours if he manages to do a drill now. He wants to sleep now.

Consumption of vegetables contributes to the intake of precious proteins and calcium. But the benefits of protein and calcium intake are rewards that are delayed and their impact is not immediately felt. Besides, the benefits are facts, not a feeling. The feeling is one of healthiness, which can be right now.

Quitting smoking because it causes cancer is a good decision. But cancer may not happen immediately, rather over a period of time. The threat of cancer, thus, may not deter people from smoking, because the reward is too far-off. Besides, there is no certainty that you will not have cancer just because you give up smoking. Right now, a cigarette is more rewarding than the reward of not getting cancer in the future. The reward of not smoking is credible, but it's both delayed and uncertain. If it can be transformed into the immediate—the reward of being a good parent or husband or wife—it has great chances of working.

The feeling of giving up smoking, the feeling of having nutritious food, the feeling of adventure and freedom, the feeling of driving a new car; these are enormously powerful emotions, and they transcend the obvious rational rewards.

The physical reward can be delayed, but the feeling is immediate and here and now. Feeling is what the people *actually* want. Feeling is assured even though the physical reward is uncertain. Most importantly, while an attribute is rational, feeling is emotional and connects with our automatic system.

If I donate money to a charitable organization to educate underprivileged children, the result is delayed and uncertain. But the feeling of helping a child is immediate and certain. It's emotional.

Feelings also get into rewards that are additional and do not depend on the action that is recommended.

The Image Matters

Physical experience flows from action. When you savour an ice cream, you click your tongue in appreciation of the taste. When you drive a car that is known for its quick acceleration, you experience a sense of excitement. When you teach students in a class and the students are responsive, you experience satisfaction and happiness over the connect you have made.

But not all feelings come from a physical experience, although that may *appear* to be the case. Smoking a certain brand of cigarette doesn't make you macho. Wearing a particular brand of clothes or possessing a high-end leather bag brand doesn't make you hip or a high-flyer. These feelings do come, but they are as a result of the image that has been created around these brands. The image gets established by the use of personalities in the advertising campaigns or those brands. Personalities that are celebrities and project the image of being macho or high-flyers.

These are perceptions that our automatic system absorbs and associates with action. Nonetheless, the image is a powerful tool of persuasion. Certain brands of watches are advertised by actors who have played the role of James Bond in 007 films. Some watches feature tennis celebrities such as Roger Federer.

The perception of a person who drives a high-end Rolls Royce, wears a Rolex or Omega watch, or prefers a Carrier air-conditioner is the image. It may be accurate or wrong, but that is immaterial to the target. When we perform a similar action—drive a Rolls Royce, wear a Rolex watch or use a Carrier air-conditioner—we feel that we are imbibing the image that has been created.

Images create stereotypes. When we wear a watch or an apparel brand that a particular celebrity is wearing, we accept the stereotypical image the advertising projects. We identify with that personality to some extent and take pride in doing what he/she does in the ad campaign.

Feelings cannot be measured because they are invisible. The invisibility makes it all the more difficult to quantify in terms of communication. The creation of an image makes feelings visible and apparent and, therefore, easier to tap into in matters of persuasion. The advertising agency—which acts as a persuader wanting you to act like its protagonist in the advertisements—wears a certain watch or patronizes a particular brand of clothes or consumes a certain brand of soft drinks.

Image is the key; which is why, when a celebrity endorsing those brands falters in his personal or professional life, the brand image gets affected as well. Tiger Woods is a good example. We get turned off and discard the products those personalities endorse; so much so that even the product manufacturers drop such personalities.

If a celebrity who has kicked the habit of drugs is also enormously successful in his career and is seen as intelligent and cool, a person who consumes drugs would be motivated to leave the bad habit. However, if the celebrity is viewed as dull and boring, the good thing that he has done, of quitting drugs, might not rub off on a teenager who could be put off by the lack lustre image.

Image Enhancement

As social animals, we want to be approved by others, liked by others and praised by others. We desire esteem, respect and adoration. We want love and affection.

When we buy healthy food, we want to be seen as part of that group of people that buys healthy food. When we walk into a general store, we pick up fresh fruit instead of ice cream because we believe that people around would notice and appreciate our choice.

We do this because we think that our action influences the impressions that others have about us. We believe that every action of ours is being noticed—what we eat, what we buy and what we wear. Though the fact is that, most of the time, nobody is noticing our acts—at least not in the judgmental way we think they do.

But this is not what the persuader would want to underline. The belief that we are being constantly seen and judged by our acts works well for the marketer (in terms of winning over a consumer) and the target (it makes him do the right thing most of the times).

The above examples are those of public image enhancements—what others think about us. There is also the self-image enhancement. At times, we act in ways that gives us a feeling of being like the celebrity endorsing a product, whether others think so or not. We buy cheese products because it makes us feel responsible towards our health, regardless of whether anybody is noticing us make the purchase in a store or not. When a mother prepares a healthy meal for her child, she does not bother about the fact that nobody is watching her in the kitchen of her home. She feels good from within that she is helping her child grow healthy.

Image enhancements work on the strength of associations. Our non-conscious automatic system associate attributes with action when we see that action being taken or projected to be taken by people whom we adore.

Because we are social animals, what people think about us, about our actions and about our behaviour matters to us. A third-party evaluation is essential to our ability to understand matters around us and make sense of them. Such is the necessity that we even personify inanimate objects like automobiles, alcohol or cigarettes.

Making sense and adjustment to the stereotypes of the people we seek to emulate becomes helpful in understanding the motives of the target, whether it is wanting someone dear to quit smoking, a child to attend school regularly or a voter to vote for a particular candidate. Positive images work in favour of the targeted action.

If we have a failed actor endorsing a car brand, there is little hope of that car doing well in the market. If we have a politician who is trained beyond redemption, there is little chance that his appeal to the voters—regardless of the carrots he dangles—is working. On the other hand, a successful actor is one whose action we emulate, whether in buying a car or a watch or a dress. When a candidate with a clean record and positive public image asks for our votes, we will more willingly offer it.

Making a choice is a matter of faith. We repose our trust in a particular brand or person, because it is not always possible to judge the product in detail. For instance, we may not know the technical specifications of a car in detail. But if a celebrity whom we trust is endorsing it, we make that leap of faith to trust that car too. The same is true of any other product. The perception, that the car is worth a buy, comes from the celebrity who tells us to buy it. If the customer wants to buy a car that makes him seem smart, he will buy a car that smart people endorse. If they want to buy a vehicle that makes them look intelligent in terms of choosing mileage over style, they will choose a car that is endorsed by an intelligent man—maybe an academic or a scholar who chooses utility over overt style.

It is for the persuader to understand what the buyer wants and what his profile is. He should then show the way to the customer. The persuader, in this case, a car salesman, must speak the customer's language—his preferences—to successfully close the deal. You are what you do, and it does not matter why you do it.

Pleasant Resorts Case

The criticality of associating an action with the feelings of a client through the image of a celebrity personality was evident in the case of Pleasant Resorts, which was looking to attract the business traveller. An advertising agency was given the job of creating the most suitable promotional campaign.

The agency understood from the beginning that convenience of location was an important factor. But then, many well-known hotels are situated in and around the same locality, say, close to the airport; and they are clustered. Thus, convenience of location could not become the basis of choice. There had to be something else. A bit of field work by the ad agency led to the conclusion that a perception about the kind of guests who stayed at Pleasant Resorts was an important factor.

But how would the perception of Pleasant Resorts be different from the other five-star hotels? All had spacious rooms. All provided clean and comfortable beds. All five-star hotels had prompt and efficient room service. The food in all of them was of high quality.

The ad agency spoke with several frequent business travellers on their perceptions about the five-star hotels conveniently located near the airport, alongside or close to Pleasant Resorts. Questions were asked on cleanliness, food, amenities such as club house, sauna, etc. The agency sought their preference.

On collating the information thus gathered, keeping in mind that the material pertained to hotels in the same price range as Pleasant Resorts and as conveniently located, it was found that the perception of a majority of travellers regarding cleanliness and such was the same for all hotels. Therefore, those perceptions were of no real use in predicting the choice of the business traveller. What stood out in the survey was the fact that the respondents reacted favourably to hotels that had the image of catering to 'sophisticated travellers'. Material rewards such as clean beds, good food and efficient services were not as motivating as the emotional reward of being seen as a sophisticated traveller.

The advertising agency then spoke to many more business travellers and concluded that travellers wanted to see themselves as 'modern travellers' and also wanted others to view them accordingly. The association between being modern and Pleasant Resorts had to be created and promoted.

Here is a nuance that needs to be grasped. If Pleasant Resorts wanted to cater to modern travellers, it would have to, of course, offer clean beds, quality food, efficient room service, etc. But rather than promote each of these attributes individually, the hotel had to package them all as an essential offering to the modern traveller. After all, one may promote comfortable beds, but that would not mean that the food is good. One can talk of quality of food but that would not implicitly mean that room service is of a high level. The package worked as clientele grew threefold.

The campaign struck upon the punch line: 'Where are you sleeping with?' The answer given was: 'With Pleasant Resorts, of course. What else did you think?'

The following advantages occur when we play upon feeling rather than just attributes, which are material in nature:

- We promise an end rather than the means.
- We get accuracy, because feelings guide us to the Revealed reason. Attributes can take us haywire.
- We can convert a delayed, and often uncertain, reward into an immediate, certain reward.
- We can exploit those rewards that do not depend on physical action.

When we use the image, we offer our target the chance to appear like the actor for others to see and an opportunity to be seen by themselves as that of the actor. Besides, we also add on a host of positives that the celebrity endorsing a brand is associated with.

8

EXPECTATION AND EXPERIENCE

How do perceptions get created in our minds? Perceptions are formed not only from the sensory data which our mind uses. What we see is important in forming perceptions, but that alone is not the contributor. Our mind mixes up inputs from our senses with our views about people, places, materials, our experiences and understandings.

Perceptions are the creature of the automatic mental system that our mind deploys, and those perceptions are guided by expectations. This is for the good because expectation enhances the process of perception and lets us experience more immediately the pleasure of the rewards. Of course, for that to happen, the stimulus that takes forward the perception matches the expectation.

Can we, then, make cornflakes taste better without really changing the cornflake? Can we make the process of voting more self-satisfying without changing the voting conditions? Can we make driving the Mercedes Benz more exciting without changing the technical specifications of the car? We can do all of the above. It is a matter of expectation matching perception. What we feel, taste, see or smell depends on what we *expect* to feel, taste, see or smell. What the eye sees, what the nose smells, what the tongue tastes and what the heart feels, is only part of what is there to the issue. Without expectation, the picture is incomplete. In other words, if we can change the expectation, we can have a new experience with the same old thing. If we expect the cornflake to taste better, it will.

Various experiments have been conducted across the world to determine and establish the link between perception and expectation. In one such experiment, children between the ages of four and six were served two servings of vegetable burgers—one came in a McDonald's packet and the other had a lesser-known outlet's label. The researchers asked the respondents as to which tasted better. A majority of the respondents opted for the McDonald's packaged burger.

All the burgers had come from McDonald's, but the children gave a thumbs down to the non-McDonald's one because they *expected* the McDonald's label to have a better tasting burger. It is this expectation that influenced the children's experience and perception. They are not influenced because they are children but because they are human. The same would be largely true in the case of adults too. The expectation of good taste from McDonald's burgers made the children feel that the taste was good.

A marketing agency discovered that consumers complained of heaviness after drinking a certain brand of soft drinks in one State. In another State, a different brand of soft drinks had resulted in a similar complaint. The situation was clear: it was not the brand that was giving headaches. If the brand was the culprit, then the same brand ought to be leading to the same complaint in other States as well. The problem was something else. The unpopularity of a particular brand was causing the headache. In other words, the brand that was unpopular was *seen* to be leading to headaches. The expectation of the brand not being good enough was causing the perception of a headache. The consumer believes that the consumption of large quantities of soft drinks of an unpopular brand gives him a headache, but the consumption of a large amount of soft drink from a popular brand does not.

If we expect something, we experience that. Psychologists have found that certain areas of our brain respond in a prejudiced manner to well-known brands. The brain parts are favourably disposed to such brands, whether in matters of taste, smell or feel. The brain does not behave as such, because it determines the difference between brands—we have seen how the burger 'tasted better' when it was labelled as McDonald's, as opposed to that same brand burger when it came with a different label. Psychologists call it the Perpetual Set. The way you see the word depends greatly on how you view your past experiences, motivations, emotions, beliefs and even your culture. If you are a student and expect a particular class to be boring, it is most likely that you will find it boring.

Who determines what is pleasurable beyond the material qualities? It is the promotional campaign that an advertising agency unleashes. If it can understand the power of expectation and taps into it, it will have a successful run. This is different from over-enhancing—of raising expectations that cannot be met. Tapping into expectations works not just for products but for nations too. Various countries have promotional campaigns to draw tourists, associating various expectations to the material things they will see. South Korea's new travel campaign: 'Feel the Rhythm of Korea'—a series of eight videos showcasing the traditional and modern facets of ten Korean destinations to an original soundtrack of K-pop and folk music—has reached 161 million views on YouTube, with numbers continuing to climb for what is possibly the most successful single global tourism recovery campaign to launch since the pandemic.

Sometimes, the expectation projected can put people off. Let's take the example of Pleasant Resorts again. Suppose it were to say that staying in their property meant freedom of body and mind. Not bad, as people do want to unwind, especially the frequent business traveller. But if the resort's advertising campaign was to show barely-clad men and women bordering on nudity, frolicking the premises, it would put off many travellers. Even the modern traveller would hesitate to stay in a resort where men and women move about in semi-naked fashion most of the time.

The Impact of 'Liking'

We normally look for or pay attention to material or information that suits our perspective. In the process, we tend to downplay those evidences that contradict our perspective. This is a selective screen at work. Any information that does not match our current perspective is blocked by the selective shield. And even if such information manages to get past that shield, we interpret it in ways that suit our perspective, our liking.

People with different perspectives can interpret the exact same data in different ways. This is very evident in politics, where a set of data is used by rival parties in different ways to promote their respective positions. The liberals and the conservatives, for instance, will see the same data in two radically different ways. In the US, the Democrats and the Republicans will clash on the same data; in Britain for instance, the Labour Party and the Conservative Party will interpret the same data in very different manners based on their liking.

When we feel a little more positively about a kind of action, whether it is voting for a candidate, buying a car or choosing a school, we look for evidence that bolsters our liking. This can even take a funny turn. For instance, if we went to a fortune-teller and he told us that the first person we meet at the turn of the road would be a super-rich man, we would look at that first person we encounter at the turn of the road as a super-rich man. Never mind if that person is dressed shabbily and is begging for alms—we will tell ourselves that clothes do not make a man. We will tell ourselves—because we already have expectations of the man being rich—that rich men do not have to dress rich to make a point. We ignore the evidence that is in front of our eyes. On the whole, however, raising the level of affection we feel for an action leads to a confirmation of our bias. Affection levels can be increased through exposure.

Psychological experiments have shown that a persistent exposure to a stimulus can lead to an increase in our affection and preference for it. It can happen to all sorts of stimuli—phrases that make no sense, calligraphy, language scripts and various other visual stimuli. We begin liking what we see repeatedly.

This happens automatically. There is no need for rational exercises or to even pay attention. Sometimes, the exposure, even if repeated, is so subtle that we don't realize its effect on us. We begin to give it our preference.

Exposure works so well because it is readily available to us. We have seen repeatedly in earlier chapters that our automatic system responds favourably to availability, to what is here and now. The impact of exposure is precisely what marketing exercises depend on. An advertising campaign with an overriding message and visuals is run for weeks and months—at times, even for years—and it results in perceptions on the target that the ad desires. That is how brand awareness is created.

Brand awareness plays a major and decisive role when inexperienced customers deliberate on products. They may not know much about the product's specifications or its special features or even the levels of its utility. They could at best have a hazy idea. But if they are aware of the brand, they are more likely to opt for that product, even when they are uneducated about it. They will then sample fewer products before making their choice, even when given a choice to test out the other brands. It was seen by market researchers that awareness of a brand made customers choose that brand even when the product was of a quality lower than what was being offered by another lesser-known brand about which the customer had no knowledge of.

Even an experienced customer finds it practically difficult to test a product before purchase. He goes with his gut feeling that if a brand is popular and known, it has to be good. And even if he were to test different brands, he might not arrive at a conclusion since all competing brands boast of nearly similar features and conveniences.

Advertising, along with brand awareness and a confirmation bias, works on the customer's mind when he tests and interprets the experience. The expectation can be enhanced by slightly increasing the affection for a product or its brand. Expectations can be enhanced also by improving the associations that come with the action. Suppose our target wants to bring about a reduction in the cost of power bills, and we are able to increase the association of using CFL bulbs with reduced power bills; we enhance the customer's expectation. If the use of CFL bulbs is not associated with lower electricity bills but with aesthetics, then the customer looking for lower bills will not be impressed by that association and is unlikely to buy CFL bulbs.

The trick is to make the desired action come easily to mind. It improves the experience by enhancing the expectation. We have to go beyond physical availability and associate the desired action with attributes, feelings or images that offer reward to the target. It not only enhances the expectation but also improves the experience.

Let us not forget that perception is a non-conscious process that the automatic system follows. A product brand may be associated with masculinity, but it can be turned gender-neutral through a change in perception. The reverse could be true too. Two-wheeler makers manufactured scooters for decades before switching to what is called the 'scooty' in some parts of the world. To begin with, it was seen as a vehicle preferred by women, teenagers or college-going female students, but perception changes happened along with some deft advertising and marketing. Today, the scooty is perceived as a convenient two-wheeler for both males and females.

It is easier to change expectations and experiences thereafter. It is relatively difficult to change an experience beforehand. Before people do what you want them to do, emphasize first on the positive qualities of the experience—thus bringing expectation to the front.

Perfume salesmen offer samples to customers to experience. Left to themselves, not many customers would take the trouble before deciding. Parents can anticipate and react to their children's food habits and change their experience, thus their preferences. You can let children see your anticipation and reaction to a particular food and make them feel the same way. While giving gifts to your partner on her birthday, you can make her sensitive in advance by pandering to her likes and quirks. If she feels that you are unsure about what to give, she is likely to be less excitable about the event.

Returning the test drive of a vehicle, you can change the outcome of the action by leading the customer to anticipate the positives of the car, such as its acceleration, braking mechanism, safety features such as air bags and seat belts at the rear, and feel of driving on the road. You have to anticipate the positive expectations—else you will not be able to meet those expectations.

One must bear in mind that the expectations and the positive outcomes must match the quality of the product you are persuading the customer to buy. If you exaggerate the expectations by being factually inaccurate, you will not enhance the experience. For instance, if you tell the customer that the acceleration is 0–80 miles an hour in ten seconds when it actually takes 20 seconds, the customer will be disappointed in a test drive. If you tell everyone that 100 people are expected at your party, when only forty are likely to show up, you will damper the expectation when the inevitable happens. The key word is 'fun' that comes from expectation. If the fun element is missing because of unfounded expectations, you will have wasted your efforts.

Also, exceptions must go beyond the sensory. How does it feel to top the class? How does it feel to drive a fast-accelerating vehicle? How does it feel to have an ice cream with a vanilla flavour? Expectations change experience. If the experience is good, the customer may not only buy from you once but again and again.

9

ADD STYLE AND ART

Persuasion is an art. The elements of persuasion, such as experiences, expectation, feeling, etc, have a better chance of working when the persuader applies the art of conversation, the art of engagement with the customer and the art of leading to inferences, in style.

Conversation

Being a form of communication, conversation must meet the criteria of communication. It must convey the message correctly and forcefully, if not gently. It must use language that is pleasant and, at the same time, persuasive. It must be shorn of arrogance and should project respect for the customer. It must be lively and exciting. After all, the idea is that the message is received positively.

The automatic system pays attention to the communication, which is a kind of promise that the persuader makes. A promise that the message is something that the target wants to receive. If that promise is broken, the purpose will not be achieved. The message must be new and fresh. If it is something that is only routinely passed over and is already known to the target, it will not be worthy of the target's consideration.

Alison Wood Brooks is an associate Professor at Harvard Business School who specializes in behavioural insights and the power of conversation. She says, 'Conversation is a profound part of the human experience. To share our ideas, thoughts, and feelings with each other, we converse face to face and remotely—via phone, email, text message, online comment boards, and in contracts. Conversations form the bedrock of our relationships and, often, function as the vehicle of productivity at work.'[16] Despite the importance of conversation, most people make conversational mistakes, even in workplaces where appropriateness matters. She points out that we 'say things we shouldn't (errors of commission) and don't say things we should (errors of omission)'.

Unfortunately, most people make conversational mistakes. This is especially true in the workplace, where norms and rules of appropriateness and professionalism matter, and issues surrounding voice and backlash abound. We say things we shouldn't (errors of commission) and don't say things we should (errors of omission).

Earlier researches on conversation was limited because conversations are difficult to capture and scrutinize. Professor Brooks uses traditional as well as modern methods such as machine learning, natural language processing, field experiments and laboratory experiments to improve conversational techniques. She has identified methods that people should use more often than they do: seeking advice, tendering apologies, revealing

---

[16]Alison Wood Brooks, 'The Psychology of Conversation', Harvard Business School, https://www.hbs.edu/faculty/Pages/item.aspx?research=7741, Accessed on 4 April 2022.

personal failures, etc. On the other hand, she has identified some tactics people use often but shouldn't, such as making inappropriate jokes at the workplace and offering backhanded compliments.

Let's take the instance of asking someone to quit smoking. To tell the person, 'You should give up smoking', is stating the obvious—something that the target already knows and understands. He must have heard it a thousand times from different people. It's a message that does not come with any meaningful expectation. You need to have something interesting to say, because if you have nothing new or interesting, the message will not be persuasive to effect a behavioural change. If there is nothing new to say, then say it the old way but in a novel manner. Add to it some information that is fresh. Talk about what your target hopes to gain by giving up smoking. He will listen to you more seriously.

The message should be based on what the target wants to hear and not on what you want to say. To do that, you have to think like the target and get into his mind, so to say. You must understand how he views the world.

We spend long hours honing the message we wish to convey. Instead, we should be opening some time in crafting a message that the target wants to hear and which will make him change his behaviour. The best conversations are those which leaves out what the target knows or can provide on his own.

Persuasion must not go overboard. There is nothing more disastrous than over-messaging, even if it is clever, amusing or appealing otherwise. If a message is all about what the sender wants to say and not about what the receiver wants to hear, and that message goes hammer and tongs, it is destined to be a certain failure.

'Stop catcalling women,' is a message that is noble in intent. After all, none can dispute with the sentiment. But's it's unlikely to click with the person getting the message—through ad campaigns, posters, roadside banners, etc. It is preachy and accusatory in tone. It results in a negative emotional response.

The issue can be better approached in a different way. Why do men catcall women? They think it is a way to display their manliness, assert their physical superiority. What if an ad campaign features celebrities that have an image of being macho, saying: 'It's cowardice, not manliness, to catcall a woman,' or 'Real men don't catcall women'? That's a lot more appealing and less preachy.

The target believes that a message it receives is the one it wants to receive. When that doesn't happen, the target feels cheated and the outcome can be quite the opposite of what is desired by the persuader.

One of the most seminal works done on the subject of conversation was by Herbert Paul Grice. His most influential contribution has been on the theory of meaning, which he began to develop in 1948. It was published in 1957. Ten years later, he expanded on the subject in his lectures delivered at Harvard. These lectures were published as 'Utterer's Meaning and Intentions'[17] and as 'Utterer's Meaning, Sentence Meaning, and Word Meaning.'[18]

He categorized meanings into 'natural' and 'non-natural'. For

---

[17] H.P. Grice, 'Utterer's Meaning and Intention', *The Philosophical Review*, Vol. 78/2, 1969, Pp- 147–77. https://doi.org/10.2307/2184179.

[18] H.P. Grice, 'Utterer's Meaning, Sentence-Meaning, and Word-Meaning', *Foundations of Language*, Vol. 4/3, 1968, Pp- 225–42. http://www.jstor.org/stable/25000329.

the first, he gave the example of 'those spots mean measles'; for the second, 'John means he will be late'. There are two types of non-natural meanings, according to him. One is the utterer's meaning—what a person means by an utterance. The other is timeless meaning—also called today as conversational meaning.

The conversational meaning is something that an audience can make out from the way something was said by a speaker rather than what was actually said literally. For instance, if a person says, 'I will be driving' when offered a drink, he means that he would not take the drink because he would be driving. There was no need to say the entire thing.

People can take offence at a speaker if the latter says too much by way of a conversation, because it would seem like the hearer does not have the capacity to understand the unsaid. Therefore, the right balance in a conversation is necessary. There is no need to communicate what is unnecessary. If Roger Federer wears a particular brand of watch and feels great, I too will feel great if I wear it; Federer does not have to tell me that. If he were to do so, I might feel slighted.

Our messaging communicates how much assistance we think the audience requires to process the information communicated. If our message is right, it connects with the target. But if our messaging is wrong, then we leave the target audience insulted and put off.

When Apple says 'Think different', it employs just the surface message. It leaves the target the space to think accordingly. Had Apple said to think this way or that way, it would seem like an imposition. In the end, it did not have—since its ad campaign featured personalities who did not tread the known path—the likes of Alfred Hitchcock, Miles Davis and others.

The ad leaves huge gaps for the target to fill, according to their perceptions, things that have not been said but implied. This approach associates people who choose Apple with independent-mindedness, innovative and, yes, different minds. Apple accepts that its audience can recognize, admire and emulate the personalities it features in its campaigns.

The crux, therefore, is that there are times when the most important part of the message is what remains best left out, not what is explicitly said.

Inference

The implicit meaning that is left out of a message establishes a rapport with the target, but it does more than just that. It leads to participation and invites inference. The inference is the conclusion the target reaches on receiving the message. If the message were to convey that conclusion in so many words, the target gets suspicious, but when he is left to himself to draw that same conclusion, it will have validity.

Messages are meant to make the target behave in a certain, positive way. We cannot have messages that tell people to try out drugs, alcohol, cigarettes or vote for corrupt politicians. Instead, we ask people to join other people who have quit smoking, don't take drugs and vote for honest and capable candidates in elections.

The target audience needs evidence: thought evaluate the action we suggest. One evidence is the message itself, when we leave out what the target must derive on his own. It's not just a literal part that the audience gets but the spirit behind those words and the context around which the message is woven. The content, the style, the sound of the words, etc. all contribute to the effect of the messaging. The inferences drawn are automatic and effortless—and often without the receiver knowing it consciously. He gets the message, whether he wants it or not.

Social psychologist Fritz Heider did pioneer work on the concepts of social perception and casual attribution. His *The Psychology of Interpersonal Relations* is his most significant contribution in the field of social psychology. It pioneered the attribution theory. The author argued that social perception followed the same rules of physical perception (that are logical). He also said that 'behaviour engulfs the field'[19].

The automatic system does not stop at logic propositions, though. The message, in its entirety and not just the logical, is the principal source of intimation to the target audience. It's the message as a whole which tells business travellers to stay at Pleasant Resorts. It talks about the people who stay at Pleasant Resorts; and it tells us about the report itself.

According to research by social psychologist Albert Mehrabian, born into an Armenian family in Iran, words account for only seven per cent of the message's ability to communicate likes or dislikes. Intonation accounted for 35 per cent, while facial expressions and other body language contributed as much as 55 per cent to the message's impact. The automatic system is better tuned than the conscious mind to grasp the subtleties of a message.

Mehrabian maintained that for an effective communication of emotions, these three parts of the message have to support one another and be 'congruent'. If a conversation ends up giving more than one message—through incongruence between the words and the action—it will confuse and irritate the receiver. For example, if a person tells you that he has no problems with you but says so by avoiding eye contact and looking unsure,

---

[19]Fritz Heider, *The Psychology of Interpersonal Relations,* Ingram short title, 2015.

the message will be not be received with trust.

Mehrabian conducted an experiment that dealt with the communication of feelings and attitudes. He said that the influence of the tone of voice and facial expression becomes effective only when the situation is ambiguous and that such ambiguity appears mostly when the words spoken are inconsistent with the tone of voice or facial expression of the speaker.

Action implies essence, regardless of the motive. The politician should act and talk what the voter would like him to be. The motivation of the political could well be different, but that will rarely matter if he communicates with honesty with the voters. Similarly, if you want a product brand to appear niche, then project it accordingly even if the product is not out of the ordinary. If you use actions to generate inferences, people will be unlikely to suspect the motive. And even if they are suspicious, they will most likely be influenced by the action.

Again, the persuader must take care to not explicitly say that the product is exclusive or it exudes masculinity or femininity. How can you claim, with conviction, that an action is fun to do? The message has to have that fun. The association of fun with a brand has to be established. Then alone will the target accept that association of reward with action.

The target makes certain assumptions on the message. It assumes that the timing, the tone, the style, fun element and the seriousness are all a reflection of the action we suggest. It must show that if the target accepts the product, it will gain those experiences. Take the example of a protest rally against intolerance. There is a placard that says, 'We are outraged.' That is extreme and may put off many people. On the other hand, if a placard says, 'We are dismayed,' it will be more acceptable. There is more reasonableness with the latter.

Engagement

One of the main goals of a persuasive message is to get the attention of the targeted individual or group. We are deluged with hundreds of advertisements on a daily basis—in the print, electronic and social media. In addition, there are persuasive messages from relatives, friends, co-workers and acquaintances. It is not possible for us to give equal or enough attention to all of them. But our eyes do hover for a moment over an interesting advertisement and then possibly, we give it greater focus. The same is true for outdoor advertisements as well.

If messages are crafted and presented in ways that are appealing and enjoyable, we get attracted to them because our non-conscious mind is instinctively drawn towards what is enjoyable and appealing.

But making a message interesting does not mean that we make it complex. In fact, various studies have revealed that the simpler the message, the more likely it is to seize the target's attention; and the more complex it becomes, the less possibility there is of making the target interested. Which is why the best tag lines or punch lines in advertisements are simple, appealing and most engaging.

The power of simplicity has been studied for ages. Ancient Greek scholars studied the most impactful ways of communicating and engaging through linguistic configurations and illustrations. Children, for instance, are drawn towards illustrated books—and so are adults for that matter. More recently, in 1996, E. McQuarrie and D.G. Mick published *Figures of Rhetoric in Advertising Language*. These two professors of marketing analysed the use of rhetorical figures in advertising and published their findings in the Journal of Consumer Research. They concluded that the manner in which a message is projected and the engagement done with the target affects the impact more than the message's propositional content. A rhetorical manner, through figures of speech for instance, conveys more forcefully a message than other words. But even figures of speech have to be simple and easily connectable to the overriding message, else it will be unintelligible to the target.[20]

Ordinarily, any speech consists of variety—of sound and style. When that variety is disrupted and we hear a regular repeat of some sounds or style, the speech gets noticed. There are two types of figures of speech that persuaders often employ. One is the unexpected regularity and the other is unexpected irregularity. 'Home Aid, that's how it's made,' is an example of the first category because it stands out for its rhyme. Although regular in syntax, it's different. An example of the unexpected irregularity is the following: 'End smoking before smoking ends you.' There is a reversal of words that brings an element of irregularity to the unexpected use of the words. It could even be a contrasting use of words, for example, 'Easy to drive, tough on the roads.'

Ordinary speech has a regularity of the use of words and phrases in the conventional way. It is not as much noticed as irregular speech. Irregularity or regularity, when unexpected, stands out. Of course, one must ensure that the use of the unexpected is not a violation of what the target wants to hear and that the audience believes that the message is what it wants to hear.

---

[20]Edward F. McQuarrie and David Glen Mick, 'Figures of Rhetoric in Advertising Language', *Journal of Consumer Research*, Vol. 22/ 4, March 1996, Pp- 424–438. https://doi.org/10.1086/209459

There are two ways to render a speech—in a hyperbolic fashion or as an understatement. Both have their uses and depend on the respective contexts. In a hyperbole, an exaggeration is resorted to in order to emphasize a point. For example, some internet providers promise 'lightning speed' of downloads. Now, that's an exaggeration. When a paint company claims to be the country's 'favourite colour', that's a hyperbole. But in both instances, the purpose is served because hyperbole underlines the emphasis of being fast in the first case and the first preference in the second.

Understatement is a way of stating something in a way that is low-key. The famous Volkswagen advertisement in which the company's car has met with a serious accident and both its occupants, completely unhurt, are seen outside discussing something. The punch line is: 'The power of German engineering.' The message, while muted, is clear: that Volkswagen's standards of safety engineering had kept them alive.

Another form of unexpected irregularity is the use of destabilization. Puns and metaphors can be used, which, read in isolation, makes no sense, but are relevant in the context they are used. For example, 'Welcome to your child's new bodyguard,' for a bandage product; or, 'Make the road your friend,' for an automobile. The receiver of a destabilization message will make sense of the words and phrases, because he relates it to the overall context in which they are employed.

Two more examples of this form of messaging are: 'My wealth is not for you to share. My ideals are,' and 'Don't fool around with my country'. At times, using hyperbole to run down hyperbole makes for fun messaging. For instance, 'Those who use hyperbole should be hanged.' It shows that it is possible to be reasonable and witty at the same time.

When people enjoy participating in a message, they will grasp and internalize it better. When things are left out in apparent messaging, the target gets into the exercise of decoding the actual message and thus feels a sense of ownership of the message. They would like to complete a thought half said. It's like the pleasure of figuring out a puzzle.

Returning to the earlier message of 'Don't fool around with my country'—what does it mean? The unsaid message is that the country is strong, equipped to ward off attacks and has a say in world affairs. It's also a warning to others to keep off. This is what the citizens of that country feel. The message does not say that the country is tough, nor does it claim that it will attack any nation that harms its self-interest. That message is implied and without resorting to rabble-rousing.

Persuasion that is done in a somewhat unexpected manner always works. We have seen above that the automatic mind loves being engaged in the game of persuasion, provided that the persuasion is done creatively. We have also understood that both understatement and hyperbole can create an impact if they are used appropriately. People are quick to draw the correct inferences if the messaging is right; if it is wrong, the wrong inferences are made.

Good messaging compliments the target, the bad one patronizes the target.

That said, crafting an effective message is easier said than done—which is why there is an army out there of experts to do it. The marketing people, the advertisers, the sales personnel—they are all involved in finding ways to create a message that hits the bull's eye.

10

THE PERSONAL TOUCH

The power of persuasion, described in the earlier chapters and how one can get that power, applies to all forms of persuasion. Understanding the human mind, human nature is the secret to effective persuasion.

Persuasion can be macro in nature, where the attempt is to change the behaviour of millions of people at the same time. An example of that is to make people buy and consume cornflakes. It can be micro in nature, targeting the behaviour of many people but few quantities at a time. An instance of that would be seeking to sell a car at a showroom. It can also be micro in nature, with an attempt to change the behaviour of an individual.

While all these forms can be approached with the methods of persuasion described in the book, different tools have to be used in these separate cases. In the macro instance, the task is to change the behaviour of large groups of people at the same time. The tools of persuasion would be price, distribution, packaging, hours of operations, location, advertising campaigns, public relations, etc. The interactions through these means are neither personal nor intimate, because the persuader does not know all these millions of people personally.

But because the target is millions of people, the chance of

success is also in the millions. Let's say that our target size for promoting cornflakes is 20 million people. If we could convince even 20 per cent of them, we would have four million new or more frequent consumers of cornflakes. That would be a huge market for the brand manufacturer.

Take another instance. There are eight million voters in a constituency. If we can swing even 30 per cent of them in favour of a candidate, it could result in a sweeping win for that candidate. If we can get even 10 per cent of the children to eat healthy food and do exercises, we could dramatically reduce the number of obese children in our society. We may fail to convince all of the target audience, but even a percentage of them chasing their behaviour would result in a success.

Macro persuasion is an occupation. We can do it for commercial gains, like the promotion of Cornflakes; or, we could do it for humane reasons, like soliciting contributions for a non-government organization engaged in providing education to children from the marginalized sections of society.

Micro persuasion can be both a job and personal. A salesman in a car dealership interacts with many people, but he has to persuade them individually. Thus, while the tools of persuasion would be the price, features, comfort and mileage, there would also be a certain amount of personal interaction that could influence sales. The salesman's attitude, his ability to send across the right message, his body language, etc. would contribute to bringing about a change in the customer's behaviour—in this case, making a purchase.

A salesman's personal conduct would also involve his ability to associate the product with what the customer wants. Is the customer looking for an exciting ride, more space and comfort, better mileage or effective after-sales-service as the key determinant to make the purchase? It is for the salesman to pry the information in indirect ways and influence the customer's behaviour. There is a personal element involved.

An insurance agent will be dealing with multiple potential clients, to whom he will be messaging some common facts—the premium, the coverage of the policy, the ease of payment methods and the returns. This is all occupational. However, the personal aspect will also be a key factor in closing the sales. Is the insurance agent a likeable person? Is his attitude friendly? Is he honest about the hidden costs, if any? Is he accessible? Is he able to convey effectively what the customer wants to hear? The same is true for a door-to-door canvasser for a political candidate.

We are in direct contact with such sales people who are looking to change behaviours of many but through one-on-one interactions with them. This lends more intimacy between the persuader and the target, which is why the personal touch becomes as important as the commercial attributes of a product or service. Every micro persuasion interaction becomes more important than a macro persuasion because, unlike in macro persuasions, a persuader does not have a million chances to succeed.

Most commercial, public service or political marketing campaigns involve a mix of macro and micro persuasions. Macro persuasion brings potential customers to shops and dealerships, while micro persuasion helps in conveying inquiries into sales. Macro persuasion may assist in making voters interested in a particular candidate, but it is the micro persuasion by door-to-door canvassers at booth levels that tilts the scale decisively in favour of that candidate.

Personal Persuasion

Pure personal persuasion is different. The target is neither millions of people at a time nor many people but one at a time. It is an individual whom we know beforehand and know well. It could be a husband whose tobacco habit you want to tackle, or a child whose ability to concentrate on his or her studies you wish to enhance. It could be the neighbour whose dog barking keeps you awake at night. Here, face to face interactions are accompanied by the fact that we know them well. That should make persuasion easy, but it doesn't. Our success rate would be either zero or 100 per cent.

When we set about to change the behaviour of individuals whom we know, it is clear that we are unhappy with their current behaviour. This brings us into conflict with such individuals and has the potential of risking our ongoing relationship with them. Our attempts would be seen as criticism and resisted. Therefore, tact is essential in making them change their behaviour.

The secrets of persuasion become even more important in such situations. We have to put our understanding of the automatic, non-conscious mind at work. We have to get into that person's mind, understand what he wants to hear and say it without causing hurt, resentment and opposition to your attempts.

As persuaders, we have to aim at the act rather than the attitude. We have to fulfil their desires rather than try to change their desires.

Act; Not Attitude

If there is a possibility to adjust the situation in a way that the desired behaviour becomes natural enough to change, without an overt attempt to affect that change on our part, we have a greater chance of success. We don't have to confront their attitude but concentrate on the act.

If a spouse has a drink and drive issue, we can deftly try to make that person use a cab or public transport by gently listing out the benefits—avoiding traffic snarls, reaching destination faster, peace of mind, savings on fuel, skirting pollution, etc. The act of changing the mode of transport serves our purpose, though it may or may not change the drink and drive attitude.

Many people like to do back-seat driving. They will sit next to the driver of a vehicle and direct him to go slow or fast, avoid this lane or take that adjacent one. They will constantly monitor the driving skills of the driver and divert his attention from his task. The attitude cannot be changed by the driver telling the back-seat driver of the perils of such behaviour or assuring him that he (the actual driver) is under control. The back-seat driver, even knowing that the actual driver is capable, would continue to offer a running commentary. It's his attitude that he cannot refrain from directing the driving. It would be a better strategy to get the back-seat driver engaged in acts that divert his attention from back-seat driving. He could be asked to check emails on his phone or read through an important document on his laptop. The back-seat driver is to be given some distraction.

You can make your child eat healthy food without criticizing his choice of junk food. Get more healthy food on the dining table and reduce the availability of junk food. Keep the refrigerator stocked with fruit juice instead of soft drinks.

Change the circumstances, and the act will follow. Try changing the attitude and you will face resentment. Most often, the best way to change behaviour is to alter the circumstances in a way that the desired action follows.

Basically, the technique is to make the personal persuasion more individual in nature. The receiver takes an active interest in persuading himself or herself to change their behaviour. It involves placing people in situations where they get motivated to persuade themselves to change. No direct attempt is made to convince anyone about anything. Self-persuasion is more effective and long-lasting than any direct form of persuasion.

Don't Change Desires; Realize Them

Whether personal or otherwise, persuasion is not about what the persuader wants. It is about what the target wants. The persuader has to talk about what the target wants and show the way to getting it. The more the persuader talks about what he wants the target to do, the more uninterested the target will be and the more obstinate he will be to change his behaviour. Persuasion is about encouraging the target to get what he wants. If the persuader adopts the 'my way or the highway' attitude, he can kiss goodbye to his chances of success.

When we tell our teenage children the merits of saving money, we not only change the situation but get to talk to them about what they want out of the savings they make. If we tell them that saving is a good habit, shows respect for money and can become useful in the future, it's not going to work. For one, the rewards we are showing are abstract. And second, it is a reward promised in the distant future, even if certain.

But if we tell our children that they can buy their favourite geared-bicycle out of their savings within three months, you have shown them a way to realize their desire. It's not the teenager's immediate desire to have a well-off retired life sometime in the future. He wants his desires fulfilled, now. No amount of rationalizing and lecturing on our part will make them change their desire. We have to understand their desire and lead them down the path. If a target gets the feeling that he is succumbing to a persuader's will or opinion, he is not going to like it and the persuader will face failure. If the persuader, however, changes the situation and shows the target how to fulfil his desire, success is more assured.

That said, personal persuasions do not always succeed. But the persuader must live with those failures, just as he can bask in the successes along the way. Latch on to the rewards that the target wants—the desires he wants fulfilled, and give up your views of what the target desires or wants. Forget about changing his attitude and concentrate on changing the act and the circumstance.

The automatic system does not yield to arguments of cold reason, regardless of how articulately it is presented. Add emotion, feeling, want, desires and rewards that the target audience nurtures.

CONCLUSION

The power of persuasion works because it addresses the automatic system inside us. The non-conscious mind of the target, when given importance, brings gains to the persuader. This has been the case for ages, but it is only in the past few decades that cutting-edge research in psychology had brought the reality home. It has made marketers, advertisers and other persuaders to acknowledge what has been the truth for centuries and to use them in their professional conduct.

Earlier, we depended on theories which emphasized on the functioning of the conscious, the reflective and the logical. It was held in those theories that man makes rational choices based on a careful evaluation of facts and evidence; that there was a well-designed flow from information, attribute to behaviour. With such theories in a dominant position, persuaders crafted their strategies under the assumption that the reflective system held the key to behavioural change.

The dominance was such that even opinions of ancient Greek rhetoricians, who dwelt on the non-conscious mind as a decision-maker, was swept aside. But some experts in the modern era, such as Dale Carnegie, held a view otherwise—based on their own experiences in the field of persuasion. Carnegie was not a psychologist but a marketing guru and a motivational speaker, and yet, he grasped the role that the automatic system played in behaviour change—in preferences, likes and dislikes—in seeking rewards and fulfilling aspirations. He intuitively understood and addressed the automatic mental system.

For a persuader to be successful, he must deal with the automatic system which thinks and acts in ways that are very different from the reflective system. The automatic system is faster and cannot be turned off. It is focused on here-and-now, demanding immediate rewards and not sometime in the future. It prefers certainty to uncertainty, even if the uncertain rewards could be bigger and the immediate rewards are smaller.

The automatic system can be persuaded to change behaviours by addressing it in its own language; logic and rationality are alien to it. That language includes:

- **Mental Availability.** The automatic system pays great attention to what easily comes to mind and gives it the most attention.
- **Association.** An idea in the mind leads to other associated ideas, and each of those, in turn, activates more such associated ideas. Associations keep happening and they cannot be stopped. They can be adjusted and managed though.
- **Action.** The automatic system considers what you do as most important. It is of little consequence as to why you do it. Action and not its motive is paramount.
- **Emotion.** The communication of desires is done through the use of emotions. Emotions can be negative (fear, repulsion, anger) or positive (love, liking, happiness, desire to possess). Both can work to the advantage of the persuader.
- **Preference and Behaviour of Others.** The mental, non-conscious mind makes use of likes and dislikes of others to formulate its own preferences. It even uses them to evaluate its own choices.

A change in the act is the ultimate goal of the persuader. The final goal is not a change in the attitude, though that may come about as a bonus. Changing the act is easier than changing an attitude. The latter is deeply ingrained while an act can be altered with a change in circumstance or by showing rewards that are possible to have and without much delay. Aspirations can be showed to be met with a change in the act.

The persuader must always talk about what the target wants, even if the target is completely sure of exactly what he wants. Once you stop trying to change what people want and try to show people how to get what they want, your message gains resonance and impact. It will sound less moralistic, less preachy and less overbearing. Only then will people listen to you with attention.

The persuader must always bear in mind that the non-conscious, automatic system is in charge with many decisions one takes. The reflective system is a fringe player here. Besides, since the automatic system is always on and cannot be switched off, it is all-pervasive.

Desires come in many shapes and sizes. The persuader must remember the following:

- **Aim for the Sky**—Don't think small. Promise to fulfil a fundamental human desire, because the other less fundamental ones have lower attraction.
- **Identify Universal Motivations**—Look for similarities in motivation across groups and use them. The similarities will usually be greater in number than the differences and can assist in a change of act.
- **Offer Immediate, Certain Rewards**—Nobody gets attracted by rewards that are promised in some distant future. Rewards

must be immediate and certain. Equally important, they must be certain and have an emotional quotient.

Never use the direct method. Don't ask people why they do what they do. Don't ask them how they choose what they choose. Don't ask them what's the most important element in their decision. This is simply people usually do not know the right answers, though they think they do. The Revealed reason comes when indirect methods are employed.

Unearth the answer using basic research methods. They can be formal or informal in nature. Understand what people who already act the way you want them to act, and associate with that action. Pick on that association, and use it on people who you target to act the way you want them to act. If that association does not work, think of something else—one where you find an overlap between act and desire.

At all times, focus on feelings. A concentration on feelings rather than on attributes enlarges the chances of success. This is because of the following reasons:

- You equip ourselves with power to promise an end rather than just the means.
- You gain accuracy because attributes alone cannot guide you to that that one right feeling. Instead, attributes can take you to many different feelings and you would be lost.
- You get to turn a delayed, uncertain though rational, benefit into an immediate and certain reward.
- You can tap into many other rewards that do not depend on the physical experience of the action that you want the target to adopt.

Once you, as a persuader, promise the feeling of participation in an appealing image of a celebrity that endorses a product or service, you end up also doing the following:

- Offer the target a chance to appear to others as the person they would like to be. This is public image enhancement.
- Give your target the opportunity to appear to themselves as the person they would like to be. This is self-image enhancement.
- Suggest a number of positives of the action naturally associated with that image.

Remember, perception is essentially a non-conscious process that the automatic system adopts. Expectations guide perceptions. You have the power to change the experience by changing the expectations. If we expect cornflakes to taste better, they will. What we see, feel, taste and smell depends, to a large extent, on what we expect to feel, taste and smell. What the eyes see is only part of what is there to be viewed. What the eyes see depends also on what the eyes expect to see. Create expectations that the eye can be made to see.

Mere communication is not the ideal way for effecting behavioural change. Instead, it is better to change the situation for a change in behaviour to happen. Also, what you say literally may not be as important as how you say it. Use the art of saying. The automatic system responds to art.

The art of conversation is needed for persuasion to eventually succeed. Make a guarantee, tacitly, that the message is one that the target wants to receive. Literal communication must be about what the target cannot provide on its own.

Persuasion can also apply the art of generating inference.

Think of the message—not so much as a content but more as the behaviour of the target that you want to change.

Finally, the art of engagement. Make your message unexpected in order to add an element of surprise, pleasure and excitement. Play around with words and phrases, use metaphors and similes appropriately.

The bottom line is: persuasion is not about convincing with reasoned argument and logic. The automatic system will reject it. You can persuade only if you speak the language of the non-conscious mind. Reasoned argument is a waste of time. The fulfilment of desires is important, not logic.